Turkey
Soup *for the*
Soul

*Tastes just like
Chicken!*

Turkey Soup *for the* Soul

Tastes just like Chicken!

Rhonda Rhea

LIFE JOURNEY®
Bringing Home the Message for Life

COOK COMMUNICATIONS MINISTRIES
Colorado Springs, Colorado • Paris, Ontario
KINGSWAY COMMUNICATIONS LTD
Eastbourne, England

Life Journey® is an imprint of
Cook Communications Ministries, Colorado Springs, Colorado 80918
Cook Communications, Paris, Ontario
Kingsway Communications, Eastbourne, England

TURKEY SOUP FOR THE SOUL
© 2004 by Rhonda Rhea

Cover Design: Marks & Whetstone

First Printing, 2004
Printed in the United States of America
2 3 4 5 6 7 8 9 10 Printing/Year 08 07 06 05 04

Library of Congress Cataloging-in-Publication Data

Rhea, Rhonda.
  Turkey soup for the soul : tastes just like chicken! / by Rhonda Rhea.
    p. cm.
  ISBN 0-7814-4130-7 (pbk.)
  1. Christian women--Religious life. I. Title.
BV4527.R49 2004
248.8'43--dc22
              2004008642

● ● ● ● ●

To my prayer warriors, whose attention to the gigantic task of covering this book and ministry with prayer has availed so much blessing; and to my girlfriends, new and "seasoned," all over the world, who continually remind me that the life of grace is so much more fun when we get to live it together.

And, as always and forever, to Richie, my friend, honey, and mentor; and to my children, Andrew, Jordan, Kaley, Allie, and Daniel, who have so sweetly and selflessly sacrificed for the book-writing cause. Thanks a million for your encouragement and support. You're the best!

contents

• • • • •

Part 1: Prayer Necessities—
Staying Spiritually Fit through Prayer

Part 2: Hope for the Directionally Impaired—
Finding Direction from the Word of God

Part 3: The Ya-Ya Ties That Bind—
Building Our Lives through Fellowship

Part 4: Putting on Our Spiritual Bifocals—
Living Life Focused on Christ

a personal note from the author

• • • • •

Pantyhose, a chocolate need, PMS—we women have a special connection. We understand those things—and, I might add, we're about the only ones who really understand the need for many shoes in many different colors. My heart's desire in sharing *Turkey Soup for the Soul* with you is to send a little note of heart-lifting laughter between girlfriends, celebrate our connection, and to provide an eternal spin or two on the important issues of life in the everyday busyness we face.

My prayer has been that this book won't be merely a few giggles and some filler squished between two covers, but that every chapter will point to Christ. Colossians 2:2–3 sums up the entire purpose: *"My purpose is that they may be encouraged in heart and united in love, so that they may have the full riches of complete understanding, in order that they may know the mystery of God, namely, Christ, in whom are hidden all the treasures of wisdom and knowledge."*

Whether it's your "comic relief" reading or your day's devotion in the midst of your own flurry of activity, it's my prayer that this book will be a blessing to you, just as you have so blessed me by choosing it. I'm praying that it will be an enjoyable read and add a little fun to your day, as well as becoming a support for you as you continue to grow in God's glorious grace! It's my pleasure to get to grow with you.

Father, I pray that you will use Turkey Soup for the Soul *to encourage each girlfriend's heart. Remind her of her preciousness to you and the exciting, fulfilling, divine calling you've given her. In the busyness of her life, may she hang on to you. Strengthen her by your might and remind her of the treasure of your loving grace for every tough moment and for every moment of rejoicing. What a special gift those moments of rejoicing are—and what a glorious gift you've given us in laughter. May you uplift her with that gift. Thank you for the work you're doing in her life. Thank you for our connection as women and for our connection in you. And thank you for allowing us this special link.*

Because of Jesus,
RHONDA RHEA

introduction

·····

A Word to My Fellow "Chicks"

A few years before my husband and I married, I moved to a new area a couple of hours away from what had always been home. I started scoping out the new turf in the most logical locale: the mall, of course. I was walking down the main drag at a pretty good clip. I popped my purse-size lotion out and started thumping the bottle so I could take care of dry hands while still mapping out the lay of the mall. Thump, thump, thump—nothing. More thumps. Still nothing. I examined the bottle and found that goofy little cardboard circle stuck over the opening. What in tarnation is that thing for anyway?

I figured a little squeeze would loosen it. But it didn't. So I gave it a big one. I mean, I really squeezed it. What was I thinking? The pressure blew the cardboard off like a baby bazooka. Giant lotion bombs were lobbed all over my face, hanging from my lashes, globbing up my hair. I looked like the Thing from Lotion Lagoon.

The worst of it was that I was alone. There was no one there to laugh with me. I had no friend to make fun of me. No one to tease me mercilessly. That made it awkward for me to laugh at myself. Laughing with a friend over a lotion explosion is a hoot. Laughing alone with lotion dripping out of your nose causes other shoppers to move swiftly to the other side of the mall. Far, far to the other side.

I felt like such a klutz. A klutz with really soft skin, but a klutz nonetheless.

If I'd had a girlfriend to laugh with me, we could've

turned it into a party. Girlfriends are great in those embarrassing klutz-type situations. A mortifying moment can become an endorphin-generator with the right company. Endorphins are those happy little chemicals in your brain that give you that feeling of being right with the world. There are two major ways to make them: vigorous exercise and laughter. Breaking out into a slick, aerobic routine alone was pretty much out. I needed a bud to laugh with.

It seems God has sort of rigged our bodies to need laughter, doesn't it? Laughter must be something he considers special, even essential. Studies continue to give us little peeks into the imaginative way he's designed us—right down to the funny bone. Some suggest that laughter stimulates our immune systems and increases our resistance to certain maladies. So actually, the kind of lotion-lobbing grace that's between the covers of this book, if you're in just the right mood, might build antibodies, reduce allergic reactions, cure the common cold, eliminate bad breath, and reduce cellulite. Okay, I added the last few for style and drama. But I still think it's safe to say that when you combine laughter and grace, you have a truly dynamite combo—and it's the Lord who powers it up. As we learn to walk in the power of the Spirit and to trust him completely, He fills us to overflowing with joy and peace and hope. Romans 15:13 says, "May the God of hope fill you with all joy and peace as you trust in him, so that you may overflow with hope by the power of the Holy Spirit."

All the overflowing peace, joy, and hope bring new courage for whatever we women face. Ring around the collar? Bring it on. Bad hair day? We can deal with that, too. Surprise facial hair? We hardly flinch. We even find courage to face the really big issues that seem mountainous—and we can face it all with a joy that can't be squelched. That's why I'm so tickled to pass on a little recipe for courage, hope, and joy through *Turkey Soup*. It's good for what ails you! We can build up our immune systems as we enjoy a chuckle or two, then build up our spiritual immune systems as we take a look at what God's Word has to say about prayer. We can giggle along as we contemplate the Bible, God's purposes, and instructions on the topics of fellowship and church. We can have a snicker or two as we learn about focusing on Christ, surrendering control to him, and serving him. We can share a little laugh as we study a little more about sharing the message of salvation and about learning to rest in Jesus and him alone.

Through it all, we can be reminded that life is in our amazing God. The more we know about him, the more we find how very trustworthy he is. The more we trust, the more joy-filled our lives become.

So sit down to a nice helping of *Turkey Soup*. It's put together with just us "chicks" in mind. Let it warm you up from the inside out!

Grace is more than a smooth move at the mall. And God's amazing grace is more than a song. A tune might come and go; his grace is forever.

part one

The Prayer Necessities

*Staying Spiritually Fit
through Prayer*

chapter one
· · · · ·
Pump It Up

It's happened to many women. I realized it had happened to me the morning I noticed my control-top pantyhose had totally lost control. It was that same uncomfortable day that I was looking at photos with friends and noticed a plump little lady wearing a suit just like mine.

I asked, "Who's that chubby woman in the suit just like … AUGH-GH-GH-GH-GH!"

After I regained consciousness, I tried to rationalize the plump look to my friends by reminding them that the camera adds ten pounds. One of them asked exactly how many cameras I had eaten. I would've chased her, but I was still wearing those control-top pantyhose. Besides the obvious out-of-control-pantyhose discomfort, there's a certain thigh-friction-spark factor to deal with when a five-foot woman with twenty extra pounds considers running in pantyhose. It was a particularly dry period here in the Midwest. Rather than endanger any of our national forests, I decided to be spiritual and let it go. My friends were deeply moved by my maturity.

Getting with the Program

Instead I was inspired to start that exercise program I'd been putting off for two decades. For all twenty of those years, about the only thing I'd exercised was my prerogative to be a computer potato. This wasn't going to be easy. I signed up for an aerobics class to add the needed accountability. Besides, it was a good excuse to buy a cute exercise outfit. My first revelation: There are no cute exercise outfits for a five-foot woman with twenty extra pounds.

You Want Me to WHAT?

From that very first day, I knew I was in trouble. You've never heard such straining, pulling, whining, and moaning in all your life. Then after I got the leotard on, they still wanted me to exercise!

My second revelation: Aerobics instructors *can* find cute exercise outfits. I decided I'd try to get in good with her, so I said, "Great outfit." She flashed a physically fit smile (even her teeth were in great shape) and bubbled, "Thanks! I made it myself! Spandex isn't nearly as hard to work with as they say." I managed to smile back, but I could tell I was losing my spirituality.

Her name was Lil. She got ready for her peppy little jumping thing at the front of the class by pretzeling herself into the 72 basic ballet movements. (I didn't know there were that many basic ballet movements, either.) My heart started racing with the shocking discovery that Lil expected me to do that, too. I thought since my heart rate was sufficiently elevated, the basic mission had been accomplished. I was ready to call it a morning and head out for a latté and croissant.

But this wisp of a spandexed woman was actually waiting for me to do those pretzel things—and follow it with something akin to running! First of all, if I could somehow get myself into one of those pretzel positions, there was no guarantee I'd ever get un-pretzeled. Secondly, she obviously knew nothing about that thigh-friction-spark dynamic (I was wearing a leotard, for Pete's sake).

I felt compelled to explain the spark risk to Lil when I inquired about her CPR certification. Even with all the laughter she didn't miss a beat in her warm-up.

Whine Along with Me . . .

I was whining long before we got to the abs stretch. She said I would find out more about my abs when we started the crunches. If that wasn't a candy bar, I didn't want to find out more.

Before it was over, I was a noodle, I reeked, and I had to face the major disappointment of finding out that the crunch thing had absolutely nothing to do with chocolate. That was painful—in oh, so many ways. On a pain scale, however, I had yet to be fully aerobically educated.

The Aftermath

Childbirth? Piece of cake. The day after the class I felt like I'd fallen into my paper shredder. I wanted to call up the instructor and complain, but I couldn't lift the phone. If I could've called, I'm sure I would have told her (in Christian love, of course) that if she ever wanted me to bend over again, she'd better be prepared to throw Ding Dongs on the floor.

There was an aerobic equation at work (it's what I call "aftermath"—the "math" that applies "after" the aerobic torture): 2 decades of sedentary existence + 1 sparking leotard + 1 pretzel*ish* instructor = 4 days of strong painkillers. I concluded that if being in shape was this painful, then I'd rather look like the plump lady in the picture who was wearing my suit. At least she was smiling.

Calisthenically Challenged

I decided to rethink my stance on fitness. (I think my stance is *sitting*.) My analysis led me to some flagrant ironies in my whole exercise philosophy. I had gone early to class to get the best parking spot so I'd save myself twenty steps to the door, then later got on the treadmill. Then I took the elevator—to get to the stair-stepper!

I considered the possibility that I might just be exercise impaired. I think, by the way, that I could gather a hefty support group for the aerobically challenged (no "hefty" pun intended—although I would plan to serve donuts at the support group meetings).

Soul Aerobics

You might be happy to know that there is a fitness program that I support, however, even more enthusiastically than a Sunday buffet. It's what I like to call "soul aerobics," and I don't ever want to be casual about my vigor and vitality in this area. Soul aerobics are the exercises we can all do to increase our spiritual strength and endurance. Giving the Lord control of our lives is where it begins—and we're all very thankful to know that it has nothing whatsoever to do with pantyhose.

Praying moment by moment is our aerobic connection, building our spiritual fortitude and fitness. "The effective, fervent prayer of a righteous man avails much" (James 5:16 NKJV). Good things are accomplished when we stay connected to the source of real strength. You can do these reps every day—without ceasing, Scripture tells us—and you never get winded.

Keeping our prayer lives keen helps us build the spiritual muscle we need for a healthy life. I want to do whatever it takes to stay spiritually fit. "For bodily exercise profits a little, but godliness is profitable for all things" (1 Tim. 4:8 NKJV).

Okay, okay, since bodily exercise does profit a little, I've decided to exercise "a little." I've chosen a nice, calm exercise bike at home. I lose a couple of pounds for every imaginary round trip from Missouri to New Jersey.

Hey, don't knock it until you've cycled a mile in my Nikes.

Exercise daily in God—no spiritual flabbiness, please! Workouts in the gymnasium are useful, but a disciplined life in God is far more so, making you fit both today and forever. You can count on this. Take it to heart. This is why we've thrown ourselves into this venture so totally. We're banking on the living God, Savior of all men and women, especially believers.

1 Timothy 4:7–10, THE MESSAGE

chapter two

· · · · ·

Can We Talk?

We women tend to be a little ... shall we say ... *wordy.* I've noticed, for instance, that I can talk mindlessly for hours on end about the latest sale at the mall, my most current hair shade, or whether or not my purse is a shape that will make my hips look smaller. Hours, I tell you. All the males in my family, however, tend to operate with some kind of word deficit—my teenage boys especially. I'm thrilled when I get more than one syllable at a time from either of them.

I'm a talker. I hope I haven't shocked anyone, but it's true. Still, even I can have a tough time carrying on any kind of meaningful conversation with teenage boys. Nevertheless, I keep trying. I'll persevere in the conversation efforts until my vocal cords will no longer twang. It's either a talking compulsion or it's a love thing. Love. Yes, that's it, I'm sure. And anytime I'm persevering out of love and manage a multi-syllabic answer or two from either son, I feel like my guys and I have really had some bonding time.

Hello? Anybody Home?

I was talking to one of the boys recently about a pretty significant development in his social life. I'll just say it was girl-related and leave it at that. Of course, I call it "talking" so that I don't have to call it "wrenching information with my verbal 'jaws of life' from a totally noncommunicative adolescent." That might make me look a bit like a conversation pit bull. I hate to admit it, but the pit bull analogy is a pretty good one when it comes to my kids. And this was one of those times I wasn't letting go until I got more info.

By the way, I mentioned to my fifteen-year-old that I decided to compare myself to a pit bull in this book, and he asked if "conversation tick" might describe my information-sucking efforts even better. He had a point. A disgusting one, but a point. It's tough to choose a favorite comparison for myself when my choices are "lock-jaw dog" or "blood-sucking insect."

Anyway, there I was, in lock-jaw/blood-sucking mode in the social life conversation. As I received somewhere around the seventeenth frustrating one-syllable answer, I finally asked, "Why is it you don't like to talk about these things?" He fought off an eye-roll and answered, "Mom, does anybody like to talk about this stuff?" My, my, has this boy got a lot to learn about women, or what?

The Other Side of the Conversation

When the kids want something, though, I must say, it's an entirely different story. I become their best friend. Suddenly there seems to be so much more to talk about. And, boy, do I milk it. Should I be bothered that our closest and lengthiest times of chatting have occurred when they had some sort of "need"? Nah, I'll take what I can get. Instead of a form of conversational bribery, I like to call it "positive verbal incenting." All part of my pit bull/tick perseverance routine.

I'm proud of the boys for every effort. I've noticed

lately they've really been making an attempt to give me a few more words each day than would be their natural tendency. Isn't that sweet? I know, too, that they're making this extra word effort out of love for me. Okay, it's out of love with a touch of patronizing. And okay, some of it might be when they need something—but I can live with that, too. I feel special when I know they've stepped outside their comfort zone just for me, need or no need.

Happy Talk

Communication is so much happier and more fulfilling when it's two-way. I can tell you from experience that those one-sided conversations leave a lot to be desired. And really, there's so much left unsaid. It's the same with our communication with our heavenly Father. Isn't it awful to think that there are things we've left unsaid to him?

He doesn't want us to pray only when we want something. He doesn't want us to merely have a grocery list kind of prayer life. He wants us to come to him for a close chat just because we love him—even when we might have to step out of our comfort zone to do it.

One-syllable answers? That might cut it with some parents, but not with our heavenly Parent. He wants us to pour out our hearts to him. Not because he needs to know what's going on in our lives. There's nothing we can tell him that he doesn't already know. But he wants us to pour our hearts out to him because we love him. People love to chat with those they love most.

That certainly doesn't mean we shouldn't ask for what we need. We're instructed to do that all through Scripture, and in fact, James 4:2 says, "You do not have, because you do not ask God." But our prayer lives need to be centered on our love for him, not centered on ourselves and our own wants in a daily "gimme" session.

Pray On

Sometimes we neglect to reserve time even for the gimmes. When we get too busy to pray, that's our huge, honking signal that we're busy enough to take seriously a need for some changes in our routine. We need to be investing more energy in our relationship with Christ than we invest in any other part of life. Even when they seem urgent, those other areas of our lives are so small, almost invisible, in comparison to our eternal relationship with the Savior.

Where should our energies go? Who should have the bulk of our zeal? Romans 12:11–12 says, "Never be lacking in zeal, but keep your spiritual fervor, serving the Lord. Be joyful in hope, patient in affliction, faithful in prayer."

When we pour our energies into keeping our connection to the Lord flourishing, the results are joyful hope, faithfulness, and patience no matter what the circumstances. Staying faithful in prayer is the bottom line. Prayer should have a prominent spot on the schedule no matter how busy we are. In fact, the busier we are, the more we need our connection to him. We need to be devoted to living our lives, busy or not, the way he wants us to. Colossians 4:2 says, "Devote yourselves to prayer."

Keep on Talking

Me? I'm determined to keep talking. I'm thrilled to know that even though I'm an incredibly wordy person,

I can't "talk out" the Lord. He never tires of listening to his children. Amazing, isn't it?

I'm determined to keep talking with my teenage boys, too. Since I'm such a talker—and since I do love those boys—I think I can do it with one vocal cord tied behind my back. I'm resolved to leave no conversational stone unturned.

In the interest of wrapping up one of the loose ends in one of those conversations, by the way, let me add that I don't think there really is a purse shape that makes my hips look smaller.

Is any one of you in trouble? He should pray. Is anyone happy? Let him sing songs of praise. Is any one of you sick? He should call the elders of the church to pray over him and anoint him with oil in the name of the Lord. And the prayer offered in faith will make the sick person well; the Lord will raise him up. If he has sinned, he will be forgiven. Therefore confess your sins to each other and pray for each other so that you may be healed. The prayer of a righteous man is powerful and effective. Elijah was a man just like us. He prayed earnestly that it would not rain, and it did not rain on the land for three and a half years. Again he prayed, and the heavens gave rain, and the earth produced its crops. My brothers, if one of you should wander from the truth and someone should bring him back, remember this: Whoever turns a sinner from the error of his way will save him from death and cover over a multitude of sins.

James 5:13–20

chapter three

• • • • •
The Power
of PMS

ll major purchases should be made while in the throes of PMS. Car salesmen have been found cowering in the fetal position, mumbling over and over, "Yes, ma'am, whatever you say, ma'am." I'm telling you, there are half-crazed women out there getting some real deals. A simple washer/dryer sale became a hormonal nightmare for one appliance salesman. He now sways all day in his special rocker, singing his little song, "If Only I'd Had It in Almond." PMS—when shopping for big dollar items, don't leave home without it.

Stay Away from Harsh Chemicals

While the power of PMS can lead to some great bargains, I've learned that there are certain things you should never do when hormonal. Hanging drapes, for instance, is a no-no. Watching your husband hang drapes—definite no-no. Hanging wallpaper falls into the same category. Suffice it to say that there's just not a lot you can hang for a few days once a month.

And do not, I repeat, do *not* decide on a new hairstyle. It's like the once-a-month bad hair gift that keeps on giving. Hormonal upheavals last a few days, but a bad do can keep you locked up inside the house for a good six weeks. I would go so far as to say that there should be a warning label on hair color boxes. Something like, "Warning: Do not use this product while operating under the influence of excessive or inadequate amounts of estrogen and/or other female chemical components. Unstable chemical mixture may have explosive results."

The Other PMS

There's a different kind of PMS. I like to think of "Prayer and Meditation in Solitude" as the PMS every woman should pursue—and not just when making major purchases. As powerful as the hormonal surge has proven to be, getting alone with the Lord in prayer and meditation has been proven throughout all of our earthly history to be the most powerful force imaginable.

Prayer isn't just placing an order or giving God a to-do list. As a matter of fact, though it certainly can, prayer isn't even required to change my situation. But prayer does something even better and something ultimately more powerful than changing my situation: Prayer changes *me*—hormones or no hormones. Prayer is the key that unlocks the power of God to work in my life. How could it get any better? Through prayer we can actually connect with the life-changing power of God! It's more explosive than any chemical combo you can think of. We're talking about power that makes the nuclear stuff look like soda pop. Hair chemicals don't begin to compare.

Power Hour

Would you like to see extraordinary things happen in your life? Try spending extraordinary time in prayer.

Jesus said, in Matthew 21:22, "If you believe, you will receive whatever you ask for in prayer." When we're investing our time in prayer, he doesn't just give us what we want and leave it at that. No, it's more powerful than that. As we spend time with him, he gives us the right kind of "wants." Philippians 2:13 says, "For it is God who works in you to will and to act according to his good purpose." He takes care of the "acting" part *and* the "willing" part. The only thing we need to take care of is the "depending on him" part.

How Do We Pray?

Praying to our heavenly Father doesn't require any special tools. It doesn't even require a certain position or a particular time of day. He hears us wherever we are and whenever we come to him, wanting with our whole hearts to connect with him.

How? Wholeheartedly. Jeremiah 29:12–13 says, "Then you will call upon me and come and pray to me, and I will listen to you. You will seek me and find me when you seek me with all your heart." First Thessalonians 5:17 spells out the when: always. "Pray continually."

Praise Him

Beginning our prayer time with praise is like dialing God's phone number. We praise God for who he is and for his awesome attributes. Psalm 92:1–2 says, "It is good to praise the LORD and make music to your name, O Most High, to proclaim your love in the morning and your faithfulness at night." I love the visual of cascading praise in Psalm 119:171 (MSG): "Let praise cascade off my lips; after all, you've taught me the truth about life!"

I was amazed when I noticed how many times God's Word tells us to "sing" his praises. He hears your praises when they're not set to music, but if you've never tried singing to him, think about giving it a try. Don't worry. He created your voice just as it is—if you're not a diva, you won't shock God. You're his precious child, and he loves to hear *your* voice singing praises to him. "Sing to the LORD, praise his name; proclaim his salvation day after day" (Ps. 96:2).

Confess

Getting sin out of the way is a crucial part of our prayer time. Psalm 66:17–20 says, "I cried out to him with my mouth; his praise was on my tongue. If I had cherished sin in my heart, the Lord would not have listened; but God has surely listened and heard my voice in prayer. Praise be to God, who has not rejected my prayer or withheld his love from me!"

Give Thanks

Thanksgiving has a high profile in every healthy prayer routine. First Thessalonians 5:18 instructs us to "give thanks in all circumstances, for this is God's will for you in Christ Jesus." How many of us are asking to know the will of God? Well, here's something that's clearly labeled as God's will for your life. Come to the Lord with a heart of gratitude.

The Bible also tells us that every gift comes from the Father. Make a point of listing those gifts in a thanks list to him.

Ask

As you pray, don't leave out the asking. It's really okay to go ahead and ask. Jesus himself told us in

Matthew 7:7–8, "Ask and it will be given to you; seek and you will find; knock and the door will be opened to you. For everyone who asks receives; he who seeks finds; and to him who knocks, the door will be opened." Pray for the needs of others, for government leaders, for your church, for people who share God's Word all over the world, for your own family, and for your needs, too. Whatever burdens you're feeling, lay them in the lap of your loving heavenly Father in prayer.

We can trade stress and worry for the peace of God, through prayer. "Do not be anxious about anything, but in everything, by prayer and petition, with thanksgiving, present your requests to God. And the peace of God, which transcends all understanding, will guard your hearts and your minds in Christ Jesus" (Phil. 4:6–7). You'll find a vital prayer life provides peace and real power like nothing else.

Get Real

Jesus told us how to pray in Matthew 6:5–8: "And when you pray, do not be like the hypocrites, for they love to pray standing in the synagogues and on the street corners to be seen by men. I tell you the truth, they have received their reward in full. But when you pray, go into your room, close the door and pray to your Father, who is unseen. Then your Father, who sees what is done in secret, will reward you. And when you pray, do not keep on babbling like pagans, for they think they will be heard because of their many words. Do not be like them, for your Father knows what you need before you ask him."

Then Jesus gave us a model prayer in verses 9–15: "This, then, is how you should pray: 'Our Father in heaven, hallowed be your name, your kingdom come, your will be done on earth as it is in heaven. Give us today our daily bread. Forgive us our debts, as we also have forgiven our debtors. And lead us not into temptation, but deliver us from the evil one.' For if you forgive men when they sin against you, your heavenly Father will also forgive you. But if you do not forgive men their sins, your Father will not forgive your sins."

Got Power?

When life seems a little powerless, maybe it's time to check the power supply. How's your prayer life? Are you plugging into the source of power? So much power, so little time! Who can even describe the mountain-moving power of a faith-filled prayer life? Jesus said in Mark 11:23–24, "I tell you the truth, if anyone says to this mountain, 'Go, throw yourself into the sea,' and does not doubt in his heart but believes that what he says will happen, it will be done for him. Therefore I tell you, whatever you ask for in prayer, believe that you have received it, and it will be yours." When we persist in getting alone with the Lord and spending time with him in prayer, we can see great things happen. It's the kind of PMS we all need.

As for the other kind of PMS, I guess we need to focus on using our power for good—even when hormones are not completely cooperating—and even when the salesman doesn't have that certain appliance in almond.

Here's what I want you to do: Find a quiet, secluded place so you won't be tempted to role-play before God. Just be there as simply and honestly as you can manage. The focus will shift from you to God, and you will begin to sense his grace.

The world is full of so-called prayer warriors who are prayer-ignorant. They're full of formulas and programs and advice, peddling techniques for getting what you want from

God. Don't fall for that nonsense. This is your Father you are dealing with, and he knows better than you what you need. With a God like this loving you, you can pray very simply. Like this:

> *Our Father in heaven,*
> *Reveal who you are.*
> *Set the world right;*
> *Do what's best—*
> > *as above, so below.*
> *Keep us alive with three square meals.*
> *Keep us forgiven with you and forgiving others.*
> *Keep us safe from ourselves and the Devil.*
> *You're in charge!*
> *You can do anything you want!*
> *You're ablaze in beauty!*
> *Yes. Yes. Yes.*

Matthew 6:6–13, THE MESSAGE

chapter four

•••••

Have I Reached the Party to Whom I Am Speaking?

I was in the middle of a live, in-studio radio interview. Everything was going great. I love it when that happens. Then, right in the middle of one of the host's questions, I heard a tinny, rinky-dink version of "Ode to Joy" coming from the other side of the studio. I love "Ode to Joy," mind you, but this was the cell-phone version—and it was coming from my purse! How could I have forgotten to turn off my phone before a live radio interview?

My phone was all the way across the room (talk about "long distance"). I was hoping we could ignore it, but the host of the show finally asked, "Is that your cell phone?" I wanted to put those giant headphones over my face and slide under the table. My response? "Well … er … uh … sorry … uh …"

My, that was professional.

Hold the Phone

I confess I really do have a few cell phone hang-ups. Or maybe I should actually have a few more "hang-ups" than I do. One of the most exasperating aspects of the cell phone dilemma is that the biggest, most bothersome phone interruptions are usually for such urgent questions as, "Mom, can we have some ice cream?" Ice cream—isn't that a great reason to blast into a live interview?

I can hardly count the tons of times I've been speaking somewhere and my favorite line has been bazookaed by the shriek of a cell phone. I can hardly count the tons of times the shriek has come from my own purse, too! How much ice cream can five kids eat?

Staying Connected

I love my cell phone. It allows me to get in touch with just about anyone just about anytime. I love it because my kids can reach me just about anytime, too. I also get frustrated with my cell phone because my kids can reach me just about anytime. "Ode to Joy" is our version of "The Song That Never Ends." Just hang around my purse for five consecutive minutes and you'll see what I mean.

My connection to the Lord, however, is a connection along a completely different "line." I can call the Father's name at every whim—even if I'm simply having an ice-cream hankering—and he is always there. No voice mail. No busy signal. It's the perfect connection.

God wants all his children to stay connected to him in prayer. First Timothy 2:8 says, "I want men everywhere to lift up holy hands in prayer." But there are things that we can do to cause connection problems between ourselves and the Lord—technical difficulties that can make our prayer lives feel like a wrong number. Here's the 411 on the prayer static.

Causes of Static

Bad connection? The problem isn't with the line. It's got to be more of a caller problem. His end of the line is always open.

Sin is the biggest cause of prayer interference. Remember Psalm 66:18? It says, "If I had cherished sin in my heart, the Lord would not have listened." It's almost inconceivable that we would allow things into our lives when we've been so plainly told that those very things will result in the Lord not listening to us. Yet it happens to all of us at some point or another. It's certainly not that he doesn't listen because he's powerless or because he just can't hear. It's not because he doesn't care, either. There's no one who loves us more. But anytime we give place to sin in our lives, we're clamping off our own line to a righteous God. The Lord is holy, holy, holy—he never ignores our sin. He doesn't wink it away or pretend he doesn't see it. If he did that, he wouldn't be the holy God that he is.

Anytime we try to ignore our sin ourselves, it zaps our relationship with him. Proverbs 15:29 (MSG) says, "GOD keeps his distance from the wicked; he closely attends to the prayers of God-loyal people." If we allow sin to take up residence in our lives, we fall right in line with the wickedly disloyal, and we distance ourselves from God. As soon as we do a spiritual cleanup, he's right there to "closely attend" our prayers again.

Unforgiveness can be a dialogue killer, too. In Matthew 6 the disciples asked Jesus to teach them how to pray. He gave them the model prayer, and as he was teaching them, he said, "For if you forgive men when they sin against you, your heavenly Father will also forgive you. But if you do not forgive men their sins, your Father will not forgive your sins" (Matt. 6:14–15). *The Message* says it this way: "In prayer there is a connection between what God does and what you do. You can't get forgiveness from God, for instance, without also forgiving others. If you refuse to do your part, you cut yourself off from God's part."

Unforgiveness will keep us separated from God—disconnected. In Mark 11:25 Jesus talked about the prayer/forgiveness connection: "And when you stand praying, if you hold anything against anyone, forgive him, so that your Father in heaven may forgive you your sins."

Can You Hear Me Now?

No need to play word games with the Lord. Go ahead. Tell him what's really on your mind. Jesus taught us not to merely repeat prayers without meaning. He wants gut-level honesty. Those long, loving conversations with him make life sweet—sweeter than ice cream—which, by the way, we're not buying anymore.

> *Come and listen, all you who fear God; let me tell you what he has done for me. I cried out to him with my mouth; his praise was on my tongue. If I had cherished sin in my heart, the Lord would not have listened; but God has surely listened and heard my voice in prayer. Praise be to God, who has not rejected my prayer or withheld his love from me!*
>
> *Psalm 66:16–20*

chapter five

· · · · ·

Urgent
Assistance
Needed

I must be an incredibly important person. I keep getting email notes from foreign diplomats and dignitaries from all over the world—and their wives, their children, their assistants, maybe a few from their housekeepers. It seems a little wrong that I delete more opportunities for wealth than any one person should even run across in a lifetime. You're not going to believe this, but not only are these important, wealthy people asking for my help with some major financial moves, but they all want to give me money! Incredible, isn't it? I had no idea I had such a widespread reputation as a trustworthy and altogether upright person. Imagine all these folks trusting little ol' me with their government futures and their financial treasures.

All I have to do is send these kind folks my bank account number, PIN, two major credit cards, and my Social Security number, and I'm in!

Hidden Treasure

Did you know God has his own special treasure hidden away in heaven?

In the book of Revelation we're clued in to a couple of amazing and precious little secrets. The first is that our prayers are like a sweet, refreshing breeze to our heavenly Father. Imagine him hanging on to our every word, relishing them, breathing them in like incense. Psalm 141:1–2 says, "O LORD, I call to you; come quickly to me. Hear my voice when I call to you. May my prayer be set before you like incense." A heartfelt prayer is perfume to God. Revelation 5:8 says, "They were holding golden bowls full of incense, which are the prayers of the saints."

That brings us to the second special secret: Prayers are never, ever deleted. The wonderful truth is that our words are more precious to the Father than we can imagine. He hangs on to them like a mom hangs her child's most special works on her refrigerator.

I'm not an important person because diplomats are clamoring to give me money. I don't have to waste time being disappointed over that one because I'm even more important than that. The Creator of the universe deems me important enough to save—and even treasure—the words I pray to him.

Treasure with Heart

I wonder if we'll get to dip in to the bowls when we get to heaven. I wonder if we'll be able to listen in on some of the Father's prayer treasure. Our prayers aren't the only treasures we can store up, but I'm just sure they're included in the treasures mentioned in Matthew 6:19–21. Jesus himself told us to invest in this kind of treasure. "Do not store up for yourselves treasures on earth, where moth and rust destroy, and where thieves break in and steal. But store up for yourselves treasures in heaven, where moth and rust do not destroy, and where thieves do not break in and steal. For where your treasure is, there your heart will be also."

I like to imagine a group of us sitting around in glory, listening to the prayers of a billion saints. I think of it as a happy session of fellowshiping together, enjoying a heavenly scrapbook of sorts of some favorite family moments. Residual prayers to a holy God ringing throughout eternity—what a sweet thought. Songs of praise that never quite play their final notes. Prayers of gratitude that offer never-ending thanks. Requests long-answered that remind us again and again of our loving Father's care for us and his powerful, abundant provision throughout our short lives on earth. Can't you imagine it as an eternal Kodak moment for the ear?

He is the loving Father who cares about every word spoken to him. I want to give him something special to hang on his refrigerator, so to speak—a special love gift from me to my Father. Didn't I already mention that I'm a talker? I wonder if a wordy woman could fill a page or two. I think I'll shoot for that. My every prayer is an investment in a forever treasure. And this time I don't have to be selfish. This treasure isn't all about me. This is treasure for my Father.

One in a Gajillion

I was a little sad when I found out that I was one of about a gajillion "trusted" people held in the confidences of all those diplomats and their wives, associates, and pets. Suddenly, I didn't feel quite so special. As a matter of fact, along with the other gajillion of you, I delete a dozen or so of those "urgent assistance needed" emails every few weeks.

That's okay. It's enough to know that I'm a special kind of "one in a gajillion" to my Father. I'm so glad he sends his "urgent assistance" anytime I need it—just because he loves me. And to think he does it all without my Social Security number.

The first thing I want you to do is pray. Pray every way you know how, for everyone you know. Pray especially for rulers and their governments to rule well so we can be quietly about our business of living simply, in humble contemplation. This is the way our Savior God wants us to live.

He wants not only us but everyone saved, you know, everyone to get to know the truth we've learned: that there's one God and only one, and one Priest-Mediator between God and us—Jesus, who offered himself in exchange for everyone held captive by sin, to set them all free. Eventually the news is going to get out. This and this only has been my appointed work: getting this news to those who have never heard of God, and explaining how it works by simple faith and plain truth.

Since prayer is at the bottom of all this, what I want mostly is for men to pray—not shaking angry fists at enemies but raising holy hands to God. And I want women to get in there with the men in humility before God, not primping before a mirror or chasing the latest fashions but doing something beautiful for God and becoming beautiful doing it.

1 Timothy 2:1–10, THE MESSAGE

part two

Hope for the Directionally Impaired

*Finding Direction
from the Word of God*

chapter six

. . . . .

On the Road Again

I was driving while talking to my sister on the phone recently, when I had to interrupt our conversation with, "Oops, I think I just left my state." Sure enough, without even trying, I had somehow made my way into Illinois. I love the Land of Lincoln, mind you, but it can be a real pain to veer there when I'm simply trying to get around in my own Show-Me State.

When it comes to directions, I truly do need someone to "show me." I seem to have an uncanny talent for getting lost. If there's an internal satellite guidance system in our brains, mine isn't receiving a signal. And my satellite doesn't have a roaming feature, either. I'm the one doing all the roaming.

You may think we have plenty of support groups, but I'm considering starting a new one. This new group would be exclusively for those of us who suffer from directional impairment. If you know your east from your west—and whatever those other two are—sorry, but you're not invited. Of course (or should I say, "off course"), even those who know left from right are a little iffy.

Hang a Right at the Dinosaur Station

However, if you're a landmark kind of driver, you just might be my kind of member. Landmark drivers write these kinds of directions: "Turn left (toward the house with the pink fence) when you see a 70-foot-high chubby guy holding a 300-pound burger, then stay on that road until you see the only building in town that's painted that yellowish shade of chartreuse. Turn toward the big flag pole with the white chipped paint and you'll come to a gas station—the kind with the cute, green, Barney-like creature on the sign. Stop there and ask for the rest of the directions."

If you've been known to spend more time in the parking lot searching for your car than you've spent inside the mall, your membership is almost guaranteed—you probably don't even need to fill out the application. If you've discovered after several hours of searching that you're not even in the right lot, you're definitely charter member material. I recently inducted my daughter, Kaley, into the new club when she came out of the bathroom and turned the wrong way—to get to her own bedroom. The gene pool is definitely flowing in her direction. I'm just a little surprised the genes found their way to the direction center of her brain without getting lost. Or do we Rhea women even have a direction center? Talk about being directionally impaired.

Need Directions?

I ran into a friend today who was suffering from a different kind of directional impairment. She was feeling joyless and a little "lost"—as if she had taken off in the wrong direction. I asked her how her time in God's Word was going. She said, "I should've known you were going to ask that—that's it, isn't it!" Then I listened as she preached herself a little sermon, after which she sort of responded to her own invitation. I talked to her a few days later and was thrilled to hear her report that she had rediscovered her joy and was back on the right road.

It's tough to stay headed in the direction of the kingdom when we're fixed on an earthly compass. If we want a joy-filled life packed with purpose, we have to study the map. *The Message* puts Psalm 119:1–6 this way: "You're blessed when you stay on course, walking steadily on the road revealed by GOD. You're blessed when you follow his directions, doing your best to find him. That's right—you don't go off on your own; you walk straight along the road he set. You, GOD, prescribed the right way to live; now you expect us to live it. Oh, that my steps might be steady, keeping to the course you set; Then I'd never have any regrets in comparing my life with your counsel." And how do we keep our bearings on the course he's set for us and live a life of no regrets? "By carefully reading the map of your Word" (v. 9 MSG).

Going Nowhere?

Staying directionally impaired results in that "lost" feeling—it's a life filled with frustration that ends up nowhere. Psalm 119:29–35 (MSG) continues with a prayer: "Barricade the road that goes Nowhere; grace me with your clear revelation. I choose the true road to Somewhere, I post your road signs at every curve and corner. I grasp and cling to whatever you tell me; GOD, don't let me down! I'll run the course you lay out for me if you'll just show me how.

"GOD, teach me lessons for living so I can stay the course. Give me insight so I can do what you tell me—

my whole life one long, obedient response. Guide me down the road of your commandments; I love traveling this freeway!"

Traveling this freeway with Map in hand sends us down happy trails. Let's determine to keep our noses in the Map and our eyes on the destination. It's the best way to avoid accidentally slipping into another state. Psalm 119:102 (MSG) says, "I never make detours from the route you laid out; you gave me such good directions."

Instead of my directionally impaired support group, I think I'll try for membership in a club that, spiritually speaking, has a perfect sense of direction—a club with God's Word as the compass. Membership does have its privileges.

Blessed are they whose ways are blameless, who walk according to the law of the LORD. Blessed are they who keep his statutes and seek him with all their heart. They do nothing wrong; they walk in his ways. You have laid down precepts that are to be fully obeyed. Oh, that my ways were steadfast in obeying your decrees! Then I would not be put to shame when I consider all your commands. I will praise you with an upright heart as I learn your righteous laws. I will obey your decrees; do not utterly forsake me.

Psalm 119:1–8

chapter seven

· · · · ·

Ya Better Believe It

Infomercials work. At least they do on my family. My kids are the worst at getting sucked into the deal of the day. They love to come running to me with their sales pitches: "Mom, we have to get the Kitchen Magic Missile! It does the work of 37 kitchen and miscellaneous household tools." I'm glad none of you can see my kitchen at this moment. It looks a little like someone already fired a kitchen missile. Direct hit. So my first question to the kids is usually something like, "Well will it clean my kitchen?" The second one is, "Will it at least make me look ten years younger?"

I have to admit, imagining 37 handy, dandy tools at work in the post-missile cleanup is tempting. It gets even better when I get to the TV just in time to discover that this Kitchen Missile slices, dices, juliennes, folds the laundry, and gets pretty good reception on most FM frequencies. *And that's not all.* The Kitchen Magic Missile makes ice cream, balances your checkbook, and with its special attachment, gives your canine a professional grooming—all while it weeds your garden.

But Wait——There's More!

Did I hear you can order the Kitchen Magic Missile and, for just the cost of shipping and handling, get the amazing Mushi knives, too? The knives are probably the most enticing. They can cut through the fender of a Buick and still slice a tomato to a thickness of less than a tenth of a centimeter. Then the amazing Mushi knives can garnish your paper-thin tomato slices with lovely radish roses. The kids love it that these knives can chop and stack a cord of wood, recycle your plastics, end world hunger, and rid us all of the dangerous effects of gingivitis.

But wait—if you call now, you can get the Kitchen Magic Missile, the amazing Mushi Mega-knife set, and you'll also get the Scalp Massager and Golf Ball Washer 2000 *absolutely free.*

Who puts these deals together? The scary part is that my kids have the 800 number memorized. That's just one of the many, many reasons kids don't have credit cards. "Operators are standing by" would tend to cause my blood pressure to rise another ten or twenty points if I thought my kids might be armed with loaded plastic. Kids and plastic would be equal to nitro and glycerin. Now, there's a combo that has the potential for being even more destructive than an armed kitchen missile.

Funny, when I give the kids little hints that some of the products on infomercials might not be everything they're cracked up to be, they respond, "But Mom, they have to be. It says so, right there on TV."

Call 1-800-TRUST-THE-WORD

There is a source you can count on for all the truth, all the time. It's not on the shopping channel, and you don't even have to pay shipping and handling. It's God's Word—and is it trustworthy? Ya better believe it! It might not be the best at slicing and dicing, but on the other hand, we're told in Hebrews 4:12, "For the word of God is living and active. Sharper than any double-edged sword, it penetrates even to dividing soul and spirit, joints and marrow; it judges the thoughts and attitudes of the heart."

Ever heard one of those kitchen tools claim to be living and active? No comparison. Not only is God's Word living and active and sharper than any double-edged Mushi knife, but it shows us black and white, right and wrong—right down to the marrow and smack dab to the very attitude of the heart.

The Word on the Word

The Bible has proven itself to be trustworthy throughout history. Psalm 119:160 (MSG) says, "Your words all add up to the sum total: Truth. Your righteous decisions are eternal." There are many fulfilled prophesies, things that were predicted that have happened exactly as they were prophesied, right down to the letter. Dozens and dozens of details were given about the birth of Jesus, for instance. All were fulfilled. What are the odds? Astronomical—no matter how you slice or dice it!

Every word of the Bible was given to us as evidence that God is real, that he loves us, and that he has special things in mind for us. The Bible is the life instruction book for every person who believes. There are well over 3,000 instances in the Old Testament alone that the Bible claims to be the Word of God. It's inspired by God and is a wondrous letter of love and hope to anyone who will take a look. The channel is always on, 24/7, every day, every season, every time you open it up and dive into its truth. Psalm 119:89–91 (MSG) says, "What you say goes, GOD, and stays, as permanent as the heavens. Your truth never goes out of fashion; it's as up-to-date as the earth when the sun comes up. Your Word and truth are dependable as ever."

Read it, study it, meditate on it, memorize it, apply it to your life. Can it change your life? Ya better believe it! And you can bank on the life-changing power of God's Word and its reliability from here to eternity—infinitely more than you can trust the Kitchen Magic Missile—operators or no operators.

How can a young man keep his way pure? By living according to your word. I seek you with all my heart; do not let me stray from your commands. I have hidden your word in my heart that I might not sin against you. Praise be to you, O LORD; teach me your decrees. With my lips I recount all the laws that come from your mouth. I rejoice in following your statutes as one rejoices in great riches. I meditate on your precepts and consider your ways; I delight in your decrees; I will not neglect your word.

Psalm 119:9–16

chapter eight
· · · · ·
The Plate-spinning Life

Everyone seems to be aiming for a more balanced life. Maybe it's because it gets about as tricky as plate-spinning. Remember the sideshow act of keeping a dozen or so plates all simultaneously spinning on those long poles? Balance was everything.

These days the buzz is all about balanced budgets, balanced tires, balanced diets, balanced exercise routines, and more. Of course to me, a fairly balanced exercise routine means you burn 300 calories on the treadmill at the fitness center, then have a 750-calorie Chocolate Blast at the ice-cream shop on the way home. I might not be the expert here, since my idea of a balanced diet is balancing the bag of chocolate almonds with a diet cola. Or maybe "balanced diet" means you eat equal amounts of potato chips and chocolate. I like them together anyway.

I wonder if we so consistently aim for balance because we've experienced the off-balance condition at its worst. I can give you a good analogy for an off-balance, out of control situation in one word: washer. When my washing machine is out of balance, the whole house becomes like a bad carnival ride. I remember the first time it happened. I thought a cement mixer was plowing through my laundry room. After I realized what had

happened—and after I sufficiently dealt with the result-
ing adrenaline overload—I readjusted the lopsided load.
All was right with the world again. At least all was right
with the laundry room again.

Spiritual Balance

Getting spiritually unbalanced causes the same kind
of unrest. We get spiritually balanced when we understand that real spiritual equilibrium comes from
understanding and applying the Word of God and by
walking in the Spirit, obeying what we've read. Want to
be steady, balanced, and renewed? Stay grounded in
God's Word. Psalm 119:114 (MSG) says, "You're my place
of quiet retreat; I wait for your Word to renew me." The
plate-spinning life can leave us stressed and agitated,
but God's Word renews. It's like stepping into a special
quiet place of retreat with the Father.

Sometimes getting balanced means we need to
"readjust the load" and make sure we're building our
lives on the sound foundation we find in the truth, the
Bible. When other activities squeeze out our time in
God's Word, it's time to regain proper balance.

Out with the Wrong, In with the Right

Real balance means the sinful stuff of our lives has to
go. We're even told what to take out of our lives and
what to put into them in Galatians 5:16–25:

So I say, live by the Spirit, and you will not grat-
ify the desires of the sinful nature. For the sinful
nature desires what is contrary to the Spirit, and
the Spirit what is contrary to the sinful nature.
They are in conflict with each other, so that you do
not do what you want. But if you are led by the
Spirit, you are not under law.

The acts of the sinful nature are obvious: sexual immorality, impurity and debauchery; idolatry and witchcraft; hatred, discord, jealousy, fits of rage, selfish ambition, dissensions, factions and envy; drunkenness, orgies, and the like. I warn you, as I did before, that those who live like this will not inherit the kingdom of God.

But the fruit of the Spirit is love, joy, peace, patience, kindness, goodness, faithfulness, gentleness and self-control. Against such things there is no law. Those who belong to Christ Jesus have crucified the sinful nature with its passions and desires. Since we live by the Spirit, let us keep in step with the Spirit.

All those hateful and evil acts throw our lives off-kilter. But when we're surrendered to what Christ wants to do and we're obeying him, he produces love, joy, peace, and all the rest. We can stay balanced by keeping in step with the Spirit. We can keep our lives in step with the Spirit by reading, obeying, and loving the Word of God.

Second Timothy 3:14–17 tells us how useful Scripture is in our lives. "But as for you, continue in what you have learned and have become convinced of, because you know those from whom you learned it, and how from infancy you have known the holy Scriptures, which are able to make you wise for salvation through faith in Christ Jesus. All Scripture is God-breathed and is useful for teaching, rebuking, correcting and training in righteousness, so that the man of God may be thoroughly equipped for every good work."

Scripture is from God, God-breathed, and it will teach us how to stay balanced. It's faithful to rebuke us as well. That means that his Word will show us when we're off-balance. It's useful for correcting, showing us how to fix the off-balance life. And God's Word is great at "training in righteousness"—training us how to keep from getting off-balance again. That leads us to the life that's right on plumb—being "thoroughly equipped for every good work"—balanced!

Aim for the Balanced Life

Let's head for balance by keeping our faces in the Word of God every day. His kind of balance makes life flourish with all the right fruit.

As for my washer, maybe I shouldn't be in such a hurry to get an off-balance laundry load resolved. After that last scare, the adrenaline rush helped me clean my whole house, write a couple of chapters, and finish all my laundry. The only problem was that I still had some adrenaline left over and the neighbors got a little worried when I started doing their laundry, too. Plate-spinners, watch out!

And so I insist—and God backs me up on this—that there be no going along with the crowd, the empty-headed, mindless crowd. They've refused for so long to deal with God that they've lost touch not only with God but with reality itself. They can't think straight anymore. Feeling no pain, they let themselves go in sexual obsession, addicted to every sort of perversion.

But that's no life for you. You learned Christ! My assumption is that you have paid careful attention to him, been well instructed in the truth precisely as we have it in Jesus. Since, then, we do not have the excuse of ignorance, everything—and I do mean everything—connected with that old way of life has to go. It's rotten through and through. Get rid of it! And then take on an entirely new way of life—a God-fashioned life, a life renewed from the inside and working itself into your conduct as God accurately reproduces his character in you.

Ephesians 4:17–24, THE MESSAGE

chapter nine
· · · · ·
Cover Story

My husband once told me that there are two kinds of people in this world. The more I thought about it, the more I realized he was right. Everyone fits into one of these two categories: "coverers" and "users."

My grandmother was a coverer. There were hand towels on my grandfather's TV chair, a blanket on the sofa—she even had special clear plastic seat covers made for her Chevy. Don't get me wrong—Grandma's house was always fun. But I can't tell you how *un*-fun it was to sit in her car in the summer. Actually, the sitting wasn't so bad. It was the getting up that was painful. I remember thinking, after I got out of the car, that I needed to reach back in and peel the rest of my legs off the plastic. I wouldn't be surprised if someone could do a skin graft with the parts of me I left on Grandma's plastic seat covers. Even on long trips, I tried not to doze off in Grandma's car. The first time it happened, between the plastic face-marks, the slobber, and the plastic-induced sweat, I woke up looking like a slimy alien. I even scared myself.

The Cover-up

I spent every summer with my grandma when I was growing up. Still, I don't think I ever saw her sofa. One of my chores at her house was to straighten the blanket that covered the sofa. When I was about twelve years old, I finally asked, "Grandma, how come the sofa has to stay covered all the time?" She said, "So it will stay nice." So I asked, "Well what good does it do to have a nice sofa that we've never seen?" She just chuckled.

By the time I finally saw Grandma's sofa, it was so out of style that it was almost back in. It was in perfect condition, but perfectly out of style. She was like that about her car seats, too. The engine in her car—with the clear plastic seat covers—finally gave out. The car had immaculate seats, but no engine.

Confessions of a User

Maybe watching Grandma encouraged me to become a user. I've never had china so good that we couldn't use it. The best towels are always out. Sadly though, it doesn't take long at all for those good towels to turn into mere strings. They look like fringe hanging from the towel bars, but at least the "good" towels are out, even if we don't have company. My furniture, too, is forever uncovered. We go through a sofa every other year or so, but we at least get to watch it disintegrate.

As a matter of fact, right before I had children I bought an off-white and light peach sofa. Gorgeous. But somewhere around the third baby, the sofa was probably about 75 percent apple juice. And that's only the "good" fluid it had absorbed. I shudder to think how many miscellaneous baby drippings were coagulating in there. Let's just say that it no longer had that "peaches and cream" look when I sent it to the curb. It looked like a sofa that had been around the block a time or two. Around the block a couple of times *in a rough neighborhood.*

If you're a coverer, you're probably making that "tsk, tsk" sound, asking why a good sofa had to die so young. Okay, you're right. It could've been saved if I had been more careful. Maybe there's some place in the middle where users and coverers can meet and find a healthy harmony—a balance somewhere this side of skin-snatching plastic covers and the other side of sofas that could start plagues.

Be Ye Users of the Word

When it comes to God's Word, though, we should all be users. No need to save the treasure of his Word for a rainy day when we can use it every day. And it's funny, because God's Word is so good at telling us what to uncover—what to take off. And there are even some coverings he's instructed us to put on. The rules are spelled out in the Word.

Colossians 3:8 tells us to get rid of "anger, rage, malice, slander, and filthy language from your lips." Then we're told, "Do not lie to each other, since you have taken off your old self with its practices and have put on the new self, which is being renewed in knowledge in the image of its Creator" (vv. 9–10).

But the Lord didn't merely tell us what to take off and then leave us coverless. (You coverers are breathing a sigh of relief, aren't you!) He told us what to put on in verses 12–15: "Therefore, as God's chosen people, holy and dearly loved, clothe yourselves with compassion, kindness, humility, gentleness and patience. Bear with each other and forgive whatever grievances you may have against one another. Forgive as the Lord forgave you. And over all these virtues put on love, which binds them all together in perfect unity. Let the peace of Christ rule in your hearts, since as members of one body you were called to peace. And be thankful."

Verse 16 pulls it all together when it says to "Let the word of Christ dwell in you richly. ..." How do we take off the old, undesirable life, and how do we put on compassion, kindness, humility, gentleness, patience, forgiveness, love, peace, and thankfulness? We cover ourselves in the Word. (Did I just become a coverer/user?) We let it live in us and become a part of us. We let it instruct us daily in what to get rid of in our lives and what to let the Lord build into our character.

Take Cover!

God's Word is our cover—in the nicest, nonplastic way. It covers us and protects us from foolishness and sin. Read it—from cover to cover!

It just hit me that I have a plastic-type cover on my Bible. Should I worry that I'm becoming my grandma? I guess I'll know for sure if I start saving those little wire bread ties and wearing my lipstick a quarter of an inch outside my lips.

On the other hand, the other day one of my kids noticed that our new sofa was already wearing out. "Mom, you know if we covered this with something you could probably keep it looking nice a lot longer." I just chuckled.

Since, then, you have been raised with Christ, set your hearts on things above, where Christ is seated at the right hand of God. Set your minds on things above, not on earthly things. For you died, and your life is now hidden with Christ in God. When Christ, who is your life, appears, then you also will appear with him in glory. Put to death, therefore, whatever belongs to your earthly nature: sexual immorality, impurity, lust, evil desires and greed, which is idolatry. Because of these, the wrath of God is coming. You used to walk in these ways, in the life you once lived. ... Let the peace of Christ rule in your hearts, since as members of one body you were called to peace. And be thankful. Let the word of Christ dwell in you richly as you teach and admonish one another with all wisdom, and as you sing psalms, hymns and spiritual songs with gratitude in your hearts to God.

Colossians 3:1–7, 15–16

chapter ten

Some-bunny Stop Me!

I wish I could say that I'm a great gardener. I would love the title of "Plant Manager." I am, however, a tad, let's say, herbally slow. I've completely given up on house plants (although I've noticed decor styles come and go, and as soon as "brown and crunchy" comes in vogue, I'm so in).

Outside, I still persevere. I plant flowers just about every year, holding out hopes that it'll be my year to flourish. This year all was going well. Then, out of the blue, I was maliciously impeded by a rabbit with a mean streak. Why couldn't he eat the weeds? But this has been some kind of gourmet, taste-discerning bunny who somehow knows how to bypass every weed that springs up so that he can make his way to every one of my favorite blossoms.

We seem to have the same tastes in flowers. The red petunias were my favorites. The difference is that I seldom *ate* them. Evidently, the red petunias are his favorite, too. He must think I've set out a colorful, bunny salad buffet. He has so appreciated the cuisine here that he's set up residence under the giant evergreen just beyond the flower garden. He's made quite the set-up for himself in there. I think he has cable.

Bunny Buffet

Every time the flowers start to come back, he takes his little buffet tray and scoops off the next round. He's even managed to buzz the grasses in our landscaping. What—he needed a side dish to go with my petunias?

Someone told me that if I put hair from our hairbrushes around the flowers, the human scent would keep him away. Sort of a bunny "brush-off," wouldn't you say? I was ready to try anything to kick the rabbit habit. But the hairbrush routine didn't seem to bother him in the least. In fact, I'm wondering if I saw him a few days later with a tiny little toupee. Leave it to that wascally wabbit to convert the shrewd brush-off into a weave for himself. I've been picturing him sporting the new do with a short, chubby paw over his mouth, snickering his cold bunny heart out at me. Am I frustrated? Just a "hare."

Where Does He Get This Stuff?

Is he getting all his instruction from the Internet? Or maybe there's some kind of bunny instruction manual that tells him how to cook up a mean spider-grass stew. Does he spend time under that big evergreen studying the fine art of distinguishing weeds from flowers, deciding which fork should rest closest to the petunia soufflé, and determining which kind of coffee should be served with the flower flambé?

Maybe what I need to do is forget the hairbrush and set up a covert mission to the evergreen to commandeer his information book.

The Non-bunny-fied Instruction Book

There's a real instruction book for those of us in the human species. It's God's Word, and it gives us everything we need for living life the way it is meant to be lived. How do we get the most out of it? We can start with a few questions:

1. *Am I spending the right amount of time in God's Word?* If you're not experiencing what the Lord has for you in his Word every day, you're missing lots of great ammo. God can use that ammo to arm you for any kind of battle your day holds. You may be missing out on a blessed provision of love, joy, or peace he would like to shower on you through his Word. We need to see the Bible as our spiritual food—essential for life! Psalm 119:20 (MSG) says, "My soul is starved and hungry, ravenous!—insatiable for your nourishing commands."

2. *What is the passage I've read really saying?* We need to be careful not to read into the Word things that are not there, while neglecting the obvious meaning the author had in mind. It's great to do some background study and find out what the passage meant to the ones to whom it was originally written.

3. *What is God saying to me through this passage?* How should I apply the passage? Is there a command to obey—something I should do that I'm not doing? Is there a sin spelled out that I need to confess and stop doing? Psalm 119:86 (MSG) says, "Everything you command is a sure thing." Is there a principle to follow? Is there a promise to claim?

4. *Is there a verse or passage I should meditate on or memorize?* There's something so very special about spending time getting God's Word all the way inside our hearts and minds. It teaches us,

equips us, strengthens our faith, gives us wisdom—even keeps us from sin. Psalm 119:11 says, "I have hidden your word in my heart that I might not sin against you."

Staying faithful in our personal Bible study time is such an effective exercise in faith-building. Psalm 119:138 (MSG) says, "You rightly instruct us in how to live ever faithful to you." Let him show you, through his Word, how to manage a faithfully fruitful and flourishing life. Would you like to see your faith "flower"? Spend time every day in the Word of God.

As for imp-bunny, he seems to be "flowering," too. Despite the fact that he's on the all-salad diet, I thought I noticed a Weight Watchers menu planner sticking out from under the evergreen.

I rejoice in following your statutes as one rejoices in great riches. I meditate on your precepts and consider your ways. I delight in your decrees; I will not neglect your word. Do good to your servant, and I will live; I will obey your word. Open my eyes that I may see wonderful things in your law. I am a stranger on earth; do not hide your commands from me. My soul is consumed with longing for your laws at all times. You rebuke the arrogant, who are cursed and who stray from your commands. Remove from me scorn and contempt, for I keep your statutes. Though rulers sit together and slander me, your servant will meditate on your decrees. Your statutes are my delight; they are my counselors.

Psalm 119:14–24

part three

The Ya-Ya Ties That Bind

*Building Our Lives
through Fellowship*

chapter eleven

· · · · ·

Ups and Downs

My kids keep asking me if I'll bounce on the new trampoline with them. I keep telling them that I can bounce without the trampoline, thank you very much. Besides I could get hurt on that thing. Not just the average compound fracture, either. You see, women around that midlife season do *not* want to sass gravity.

Case in point: Before approaching that mid-season of life, we can spot a friend some distance away and give a big, friendly wave. Not so as we approach forty. I've noticed the last few years when I give one of those big waves, the hand part of the wave is long over before that fluttery stuff that used to be my upper arm stops waving. No one wants to be that friendly.

"New Wave"

I now do the forty*ish* wave. For those of you who aren't there yet, here are the instructions: Raise arm until elbow is almost even with shoulder. While careful to keep all of upper arm stationary, wiggle fingers (and only fingers) vigorously in a friendly fashion. Slowly and carefully lower arm. If no part of you has slapped another, successful forty*ish* wave has been accomplished.

How exasperating that even a wave has become more complicated. How can I get on a trampoline with that kind of instability? What if, while my feet are touching the trampoline, the rest of me is still in the air? Couldn't I get hurt when all that stuff is coming down and the rest of me is flying back up? I could meet myself coming and going. I'd sooner look into atomsplitting. It might even be safer. One rogue upper arm could put an eye out. We won't even talk about what a thigh could do.

Someone suggested I might consider using something like duct tape on all those "not-so-stationary-as-they-used-to-be" parts. I was afraid that could require an awful lot of duct tape. I don't think I ever want to be quite that silver. The last thing I want is to find my picture on the front page of *The National Informer* under "UFO Has Neighborhood Up in the Air." I would hate to think I could be responsible for some sort of interplanetary war.

The Upside

It's one more reminder that life definitely has its ups and downs. Let me bounce this idea off of you: For every "down," God gives us an opportunity to be someone else's "up." Second Corinthians 1:3–5 says, "Praise be to the God and Father of our Lord Jesus Christ, the Father of compassion and the God of all comfort, who comforts us in all our troubles, so that we can comfort those in any trouble with the comfort we ourselves have received from God. For just as the sufferings of Christ flow over into our lives, so also through Christ our comfort overflows."

Isn't it amazing that the Lord can use our down

times to help others in theirs? And according to this passage, for every down we suffer, Jesus gives a comfort that reaches so much deeper than the down. His love and comfort reach beyond any hurt. Psalm 34:17–20 says, "The righteous cry out, and the LORD hears them; he delivers them from all their troubles. The LORD is close to the brokenhearted and saves those who are crushed in spirit. A righteous man may have many troubles, but the LORD delivers him from them all; he protects all his bones, not one of them will be broken."

We can't come up with a bad experience that's bigger than his comfort. No matter what we suffer, it's covered. Okay, it's out of context, but did I see a delivery from broken bones? Even a trampoline triple compound fracture! Covered! The comfort we have because of Christ—the one who gives us eternal deliverance—is big enough to cover it all. Not only cover it, fill it. Not only fill it, but overflow it!

Springing Comfort

Knowing the Father of Compassion is ready with comfort in mass quantity can add a little bounce to any day. The good kind of bounce. And knowing the Lord is working in our lives through our valleys—and that he can use those valleys to help others—puts an entirely new spin on the down times we suffer. Second Corinthians 4:15–18 says, "All this is for your benefit, so that the grace that is reaching more and more people may cause thanksgiving to overflow to the glory of God. Therefore we do not lose heart. Though outwardly we are wasting away, yet inwardly we are being renewed day by day. For our light and momentary troubles are achieving for us an eternal glory that far outweighs them all. So we fix our eyes not on what is seen, but on what is unseen. For what is seen is temporary, but what is unseen is eternal." See? It *does* say overflow! It's an overflow right into the glory of God.

We can have confidence that these temporary bumps and bruises are leading up to "an eternal glory that far outweighs them all." It's one of those precious times when we can consider the word "outweigh" and still think good thoughts. The entire message is one that's "uplifting" in the most thorough and eternal way—and it's a message that's guaranteed to put a bounce in your step. No duct tape required.

All praise to the God and Father of our Master, Jesus the Messiah! Father of all mercy! God of all healing counsel! He comes alongside us when we go through hard times, and before you know it, he brings us alongside someone else who is going through hard times so that we can be there for that person just as God was there for us. We have plenty of hard times that come from following the Messiah, but no more so than the good times of his healing comfort—we get a full measure of that, too.

2 Corinthians 1:3–5, THE MESSAGE

chapter twelve

Diet Church

Interested in a new strategy for the church? What about a move toward "light church." Not light as in letting your light shine before men. I mean light as in "less filling."

This new church could sport reclining pews equipped with remote control (go ahead—change the volume of your music guy). Ushers could offer peanuts and your choice of beverage so that you're not distracted by thoughts of the one o'clock Sunday buffet.

"Full-service" Service

Do you suppose there really are people who want to think of a worship service less as worship and would like to see a church that focuses more on the service part? Are there people out there hunting for a kind of a "full-service" service? Maybe there are those who would like it if, in addition to the fresh-cut flowers at the front of the auditorium, we could also find numbered seats all ready for us. Register, get a number, and check into your spot. There's nothing like a mint on your pew and having someone turn open your hymnal for you. Valet parking might be a nice touch, too.

Instead of coming forward to make commitments, ushers on roller skates could come to our seats. (Requests would be filled in the order received.) But folks would still have to walk from the car to the pew, and then back again. So how about a drive-through window? You could choose a topic from the menu, order, then pay your tithe at the window, pick up your "sermon-in-a-minute" tape, and be on your way. I can see the ad now: "Church in 30 minutes or less, or it's free!"

For those needing an alternative style—and just in case the whole drive-through scene might be too demanding—how about "Fairway Church of the Eighteenth Hole"? If we held services on the fairway and the invitation on the green, can you imagine the great response we'd see if we gave an altar call?

We could call it "Church—the easy way."

A More Excellent Way

But Jesus didn't call us to an easy way. He called us to a "most excellent way" in 1 Corinthians 12:31. Then he gave us 1 Corinthians 13—the Love Chapter.

A church ministry without Jesus' kind of love is really no ministry at all. It's an experience that you probably can really pick up just as well at a drive-through.

But the Lord's plan for his church includes loving each other, sharing with each other, and bearing with one another. Real church involves people. It involves loving them. It involves work—even sacrifice. And each one's sacrifice is vital.

Ephesians 4:16 says, "From him [Christ] the whole body, joined and held together by every supporting ligament, grows and builds itself up in love, as each part does its work."

The Message puts it like this: "We take our lead from Christ, who is the source of everything we do. He keeps us in step with each other. His very breath and blood flow through us, nourishing us so that we will grow up healthy in God, robust in love" (vv. 15–16).

To be a healthy, growing follower of Christ, we need to be in step with other Christians. It's Christ inside each of us that gives us the connection we need to stay in step. And it's Christ in us that grows us up and helps us to learn to love others with the same kind of unselfish, "robust" love Jesus has for us.

Don't Give Up

If you've been out of the church habit for a while, or if you're having a tough time searching for a good one and you're tempted to give up, keep in mind that Jesus truly didn't call us to an easy way. In any church situation, you'll find a person or two who is especially tough to love. You might even find skirmishes in the church. I guarantee you'll find areas of imperfection in every church this side of heaven. Selfishness will tell you to give it up. But listen to God's Word instead. It says in Hebrews 10:24–25, "And let us consider how we may spur one another on toward love and good deeds. Let us not give up meeting together, as some are in the habit of doing, but let us encourage one another—and all the more as you see the Day approaching."

Tough? It sure can be. Worth it? Always. If you want to live a life of obedience, you'll need to plug yourself into a Bible-believing church where you can grow in Christ, and—maybe most importantly—so you can serve.

That old answer, "I don't go to church because it's full of hypocrites" doesn't really cut it. The fact is, the church isn't only full of hypocrites, it's full of every other kind of sinner too. As a matter of fact, you won't find a single person there who isn't a sinner. But shouldn't that make us feel a little more like we fit in? Only the perfect folks need a perfect church, right?

The Ultimate Filling

A church that's less filling? Nah. We're called to be filled—completely filled with the Holy Spirit of God. Can you imagine a Ding Dong with no filling? I might cry just thinking about it. It's even worse without the Holy Spirit. And that diet church thing will leave you just as empty. Where's the filling? In Jesus! And in the words of that profound cupcake commercial: "Now that's the stuff!"

If I speak with human eloquence and angelic ecstasy but don't love, I'm nothing but the creaking of a rusty gate. If I speak God's Word with power, revealing all his mysteries and making everything plain as day, and if I have faith that says to a mountain, "Jump," and it jumps, but I don't love, I'm nothing.

If I give everything I own to the poor and even go to the stake to be burned as a martyr, but I don't love, I've gotten nowhere. So, no matter what I say, what I believe, and what I do, I'm bankrupt without love.

Love never gives up.
Love cares more for others than for self.
Love doesn't want what it doesn't have.
Love doesn't strut,
Doesn't have a swelled head,
Doesn't force itself on others,
Isn't always "me first,"
Doesn't fly off the handle,
Doesn't keep score of the sins of others,
Doesn't revel when others grovel,
Takes pleasure in the flowering of truth,
Puts up with anything,
Trusts God always,
Always looks for the best,

Never looks back,
But keeps going to the end.
Love never dies. ...
Trust steadily in God, hope unswervingly, love extrav-
agantly. And the best of the three is love.

1 Corinthians 13:1–8, 13, THE MESSAGE

chapter thirteen

·····

The Last Laugh

y husband preaches three services every Sunday morning. Every Sunday after the last service, his brain predictably shifts into a state just this side of a coma. It's like seeing his screen saver kick on—the brain parts are still working, but there doesn't seem to be any real activity. I've learned not to give him any kind of information he's really going to need until at least 3:00 P.M.

I can always tell he's slipped into Post-Traumatic Sermon Syndrome when I ask where he'd like to go for lunch and he answers, "Forty-seven." Yes, he's really and truly given me that answer. More than once. One time we even caught him trying to order at the McDonald's drive-through by speaking into their trash can.

Of course, it's a great time to ask him for something I want. A simple "Yes, Honey, you told me I could when I asked you last Sunday after church," and I can get away with just about anything. Okay, that's a little joke. I get away with things without resorting to capitalizing on his hypnotic state.

My favorite screen-saver moment happened one Sunday afternoon at Taco Bell. Richie had freshly entered into PTSS mode—I was just pleased he was able to place his order. But when it came time to pay, he didn't have his special discount tag he keeps on his key chain. When you take a family of seven out to eat, you want to make sure you get every discount you can. So he asked our fifteen-year-old son to see if he left his keys in the car. Jordan came back from the car wearing an interesting smirk. He said, "Dad, not only did you leave your keys in the car—you left the car *running.*" We all howled, though I think I was the loudest.

Tell It Again

Every time we ran into someone we knew over the next month, I'd beg Richie, "Oh, please let me tell the Taco Bell story. Please, please, *please.*" He would roll his eyes and say something like, "Well, if you just have to." I always had to.

About a month later, it came to a sad end. I was loading my bags into the minivan after a quick stop at Wal-Mart. It was one of those hot July days. My shoes where sort of oozing into the sizzling pavement. I thought I'd let the car cool off while I finished unloading, so I dropped my purse in the back seat and squeezed through to start up the van. (You can see where this is going, can't you?) I finished unloading, slammed the door, then realized I had locked myself out of my running car! I peered through the window. Yep, there was my purse. Cell phone, too. Everything I needed was in there—except ME!

Crow for Lunch, Anyone?

I hesitate to tell you about my phone call to Richie's secretary, but let me just say that the ladies at the Wal-Mart jewelry counter heard something like this:

"Janet, I'm at Wal-Mart and my phone is locked in

my car. And my purse is in there, too. And the keys. And, oh yeah, the car is running.

"Okay, Janet, stop laughing. And please tell my husband to get all his laughing over and done with before he gets here, too.

"What do you mean 'how will he find me'?

"Okay, sure, Janet, go ahead and tell him to look for the woman in the parking lot with egg on her face." Janet has just a little bit of a mischievous streak. I've always admired that about her.

I hadn't waited long when I saw Richie's car pulling into the lot. I saw a shining glow first. It was teeth. I can't remember the last time I saw a smile that big.

All I could say as I peeled my shoes off the parking lot was, "Boy, am I going to miss telling that Taco Bell story."

In-Your-Face Judgment

There are passages in Scripture that are related to that kind of boomerang fun-poking. If you judge others, you'll find that judgment coming right back around and smacking you in the head.

Jesus made it plain in Matthew 7:1–5 when he said, "Do not judge, or you too will be judged. For in the same way you judge others, you will be judged, and with the measure you use, it will be measured to you. Why do you look at the speck of sawdust in your brother's eye and pay no attention to the plank in your own eye? How can you say to your brother, 'Let me take the speck out of your eye,' when all the time there is a plank in your own eye? You hypocrite, first take the plank out of your own eye, and then you will see clearly to remove the speck from your brother's eye."

Luke 6:37 in *The Message* puts it this way: "Don't pick on people, jump on their failures, criticize their faults—unless, of course, you want the same treatment. Don't condemn those who are down; that hardness can boomerang. Be easy on people; you'll find life a lot easier."

The principle is clear. At the point we think we have the right to condemn someone else, we'd better duck! That judgment has a kick. A critical, condemning spirit results in losing sight of another person's strengths, loss of friendships, and a shortfall in our overall fruitfulness in life. It's a bad choice from any direction.

Here Comes the Judge

James 4:12 states, "There is only one Lawgiver and Judge, the one who is able to save and destroy. But you—who are you to judge your neighbor?"

Only one is really worthy to judge. In John 8:16, Jesus said, "But if I do judge, my decisions are right, because I am not alone. I stand with the Father, who sent me." If, however, you lovingly and biblically confront someone who's involved in something that's clearly spelled out in Scripture as sin, that person may certainly feel judged. But if God has already judged that person's actions as sin, it's really not your judgment call at all—it's God's. It's okay—even commanded—that we lovingly confront those things God has already judged as sin. We need to make sure we do it, however, without a telephone pole in the eye.

Learning to see people the way Jesus does and learning to love them the way he does is the way to know when to confront a friend and when to come alongside and help. Learning to love the Jesus way can help us stay away from a judgmental spirit.

I would say that it's a "key" to right living, but that might remind me of the Wal-Mart incident.

For this very reason, Christ died and returned to life so that he might be the Lord of both the dead and the living. You, then, why do you judge your brother? Or why do you look down on your brother? For we will all stand before God's judgment seat. It is written: "'As surely as I live,' says the Lord, 'every knee will bow before me; every tongue will confess to God.'" So then, each of us will give an account of himself to God. Therefore let us stop passing judgment on one another. Instead, make up your mind not to put any stumbling block or obstacle in your brother's way.

Romans 14:9–13

chapter fourteen
Risk Ski Business

I'll never forget my first ski experience. My husband was long gone—gracefully bobbing and weaving down all the toughest slopes. I spent a big part of the morning trying to force those inhumanly slanted ski boots onto feet that weren't built on an angle. I could see from the get-go that this wasn't going to be easy.

It took me a good hour just to get to the ski school. I fell so many times I wondered if it might be better to wear the skis on my rear end. The frustrating part was that it would take only a split second to fall. But then the fall was followed by twenty minutes of trying to get back up—writhing, whining, squirming, and thrashing around. I had never in my life looked so ridiculous. Of course, the day wasn't over. Funny, I thought I was going to ski school. I didn't remember signing up for humility school. Tiny kids shorter than my skis kept zipping past me, darting in and out. They didn't even have poles. They would glance back at me, watching me use my poles as crutches and grin. I don't think they were being friendly.

Which Way to Ski Lodge School?

By the time I made it to the class I had just about decided that I was called to be a lodge person. Every stereotypical visual of a ski vacation involves a large mug of hot chocolate, a roaring fire, and a comfy sofa. Someone had to keep the stereotype alive, right? I wanted to volunteer. Still, a ski school drop-out? That didn't seem right, either. I set my goal: Go ahead and go—survive ski school, then reward myself with a big mug of hot chocolate, a big novel, and a big overstuffed chair in front of a big fire. Big mistake.

Dear Old Golden Fool Days

I was a little nervous about ski school, though the first part of the instruction seemed relatively harmless. On skis. Off skis. I could handle that—especially the "off" part. But then the instructor added in the science of movement. Alas, more writhing, squirming, and thrashing. Am I the only ski school student who has come close to not graduating?

We traveled to a little clearing for more instruction. Our instructor taught us a few more of the basics, then she said we would be traveling to the bunny slope. I had never heard of any ski-related deaths occurring on a bunny slope. It sounded safe enough.

She said she wanted us to travel across a place that was "a little tricky" to get to a bunny slope that we were just going to love. I had news for her. It wasn't a "little" tricky, and I was *not* going to love it. We had to ski through a pit she called a "dip" and down a cliff she called a "hill." I wanted to quit, but by that time I didn't even know how to get back to the lodge. Ah, the lodge. I kept telling myself that if I could just get through this ski boot camp that I could park myself in the lodge and spend a ski vacation the way a couch potato is meant to. I set a goal: Ski through her dip/abyss and down her hill/mountain without falling. I knew every fall would mean another twenty minutes of snow-related, convulsive laughter that would keep me away from the lodge that much longer.

I pushed off in pretty good form, but somewhere near the crater, my skis took total control. I knew if I fell while trapped in the chasm, I could writhe there for the rest of our vacation. *Don't fall,* I told myself. *Just don't fall.*

By God's grace, I made it over hill and dale, but as I was nearing the instructor, my skis crossed. I missed her by inches (I think it sparked a spiritual revival in her life) and came to the most inelegant stop you've ever seen. The top half of my body fell forward, but my sheer determination not to fall (and maybe an angel or two working overtime) kept me upright from the waist down. My knees were about two feet apart, skis still crossed, my gloves were in the snow, my rear in the air. I looked so outlandishly absurd that someone I didn't even know took my picture! Really!

Picture-Perfect Moment

I was just glad that I could save face, so to speak. The photographer took the photo from the back. I was holding my head up just enough that the photographer could only get my chin between my knees—my face would've been nowhere in the picture. And it's not like someone would ever be able to identify me just by the ski clothes. After all, I was *never* putting them on again.

When I finally made it back to the lodge (otherwise known as "paradise"), I gave my friends a good laugh with my tales of danger and agony on the slopes. The next day, of course, I learned that the agony of defeat had a lot more to it than just a big dose of humility. Somewhere in that one day of skiing I had managed to use muscles I didn't even know I had. Even my mug-lifting muscles were smarting. My friends laughed about that, too.

See What Develops

Isn't it interesting that every difficulty becomes instantly more bearable when you share it with a friend? For every humbling Kodak moment, God makes possible a moment of closeness with a bud.

Need a friend? Try *becoming* one to someone else. We're instructed all through Scripture to actively love others. First Peter 4:8 says, "Above all, love each other deeply, because love covers over a multitude of sins." "Above all," it says. It's one of the highest (ski-mountainously high), most imperative commands we have! Above all, we're to love each other "deeply." Deeper than any snow chasm. As we love in the highest and deepest ways, we're steered clear of a lot of sin traps that might otherwise snag us. When we're energetically loving each other, we're pleasing our Father.

The next verse in 1 Peter 4 instructs us to "Offer hospitality to one another without grumbling" (v. 9). Offering hospitality to a friend might sometimes require a ton of energy—more energy than a day of ski school. But we're blessed when we do it anyway, and do it with love, without grouching.

We can develop good friends as we learn to put our own wants aside and unselfishly concentrate on the needs of others. Philippians 2:3–4 tells us to "Do nothing out of selfish ambition or vain conceit, but in humility consider others better than yourselves. Each of you should look not only to your own interests, but also to the interests of others." Risky business? Yes. But, oh, so worth it!

There are so many friendship-building helps in the Bible. We're told, for instance, that loving a friend is not just a one-time thing—like my ski trip. We're instructed to persevere in friendships. Hebrews 13:1 says to "Keep on loving each other." We're even told what kind of friendships *not* to build. Second Corinthians 6:14 says, "Do not be yoked together with unbelievers. For what do righteousness and wickedness have in common? Or what fellowship can light have with darkness?" It's okay to build acquaintances with people who don't know the Lord. That's how we take his light into the darkness. But our closest, most intimate friendships should be with those who love the light and who can fellowship in the light with us. Our dearest friendships should be with believers who will encourage us to be just the light the Lord wants us to be.

Girls' Ski-night Out

Let me encourage you to reach out and make some new friends. Put some extra work into the friendships you already have. Check out the next girls' night out—maybe even the next ski trip. Even if you don't love the skiing, you just might get to know some friends on a whole new level. However, if you happen to pick up a ski magazine while you're there and you find a bright blue rear end on the cover, I'm sure it's no one you know.

If you have any encouragement from being united with Christ, if any comfort from his love, if any fellowship with the Spirit, if any tenderness and compassion, then make my joy complete by being like-minded, having the same love, being one in spirit and purpose. Do nothing out of selfish ambition or vain conceit, but in humility consider others better than yourselves. Each of you should look not only to your own interests, but also to the interests of others. Your attitude should be the same as that of Christ Jesus: Who, being in very nature God, did not consider equality with God something to be grasped, but made himself nothing, taking the very nature of a servant, being made in human likeness. And being found in appearance as a man, he humbled himself and became obedient to death—even death on a cross! Therefore God exalted him to the highest place and gave him the name that is above every name, that at the name of Jesus every knee should bow, in heaven and on earth and under the earth, and every tongue confess that Jesus Christ is Lord, to the glory of God the Father.

Therefore, my dear friends, as you have always obeyed— not only in my presence, but now much more in my absence—continue to work out your salvation with fear and trembling, for it is God who works in you to will and to act according to his good purpose. Do everything without complaining or arguing, so that you may become blameless and pure, children of God without fault in a crooked and depraved generation, in which you shine like stars in the universe as you hold out the word of life—in order that I may boast on the day of Christ that I did not run or labor for nothing.

Philippians 2:1–16

chapter fifteen

· · · · ·

Showers of Mercy

It was the first house we'd ever owned that we saw go up from ground to roof. Just before we took possession, we did a walk-through with a couple of representatives from the builder's office. I didn't want them to think I didn't know my way around new construction. Shouldn't they be impressed that I had worked around that kind of stuff for three whole years? I could almost build it myself, couldn't I? Maybe I could impress them further if I told them I've actually *lived* in houses my entire life. I wanted these house pros to know they were dealing with one house-savvy kind of gal.

Yessiree, I was determined not to neglect a single detail. I opened every drawer, tugged every knob, inspected every wall—nothing was getting by my construction-educated watchdog eye. I felt sort of a Ralph Nader*ish* power rush.

I turned on the kitchen sink to make sure the water ran in an acceptable manner. Check. Then I pulled out the sink sprayer and scrutinized it like I knew what I was doing. Of course, I had to squeeze it to make sure it would really squirt. Thoroughness always pays off.

And pay off it did. You see, it happened that I forgot I was pointing the thing right at my head. I caught the entire power squirt from the superbly functioning sink sprayer right smack in the face!

Is That a Drip?

Well, well, well. Didn't I look professional and on top of things? Nope, these folks weren't going to be able to get away with anything with this sharp cookie on the walk-through watch. Okay, Ralph Nader I wasn't—though I must say my wet hair had a bit of a Nader look.

I'm not sure if the walk-through people missed it or if they were just being kind to help me save face—save mascara-streaked face. Or maybe they had to leave the room because they didn't want me to see them laughing their noticeably dry little heads off. Whichever—it didn't matter. I was just thankful they went to another room with my husband. I considered it mercy that I got to try to make a few face repairs, even though I had to endure the rest of the walk-through with my bangs juiced back. The part in my hair suddenly looked four inches wider. It was like Moses had done a tiny version of the Red-Sea-thing down the middle of my head. Sadly, I couldn't blame Moses for this one. I had done more than my part, as it were.

Snap Out of It!

The squirt in the face was a humbling wake-up call. What was I thinking? Who did I think I was? What was I trying to prove? Maybe I wanted to impress the folks from the builder's office and convince them that I didn't really need them. Why? And guess what? I proved the exact opposite. For Pete's sake, I couldn't even operate the sink! The builder folks were actually there to help me, and after I was snapped (squirted?) back to reality, I realized that.

God sends people into our lives to help us. Relationships are his plan. Consider how much of the Bible is dedicated to relationships. That tells me a couple of things: (1) relationships are very important to the Father, and (2) the fact that they require so much instruction means that relationships are not always going to be easy. Mercy, love, forgiveness, kindness, concern, and loads of patience are essential.

If we did a spiritual walk-through of our lives, searching out any relationship problems, what would we find? Any hidden surprises waiting to spew?

No Divisions

If you're letting petty squabbles keep you at arm's length from those you should be loving, it's time to rethink your relationship situation. It's that kind of pride that ends up in ugly divisions. Yes, like the one in my hair on walk-through day.

Scripture consistently teaches us that we need each other and that we should not let divisions happen. What's the opposite of division? Coming together, humbly loving and forgiving each other. First Thessalonians 5:11 says, "Therefore encourage one another and build each other up, just as in fact you are doing."

If you're wondering where to learn how to build others up and how to love people the way the Lord intended, you can start by looking no further than the Holy Spirit, who lives right inside you! When you allow him to work in your life, he's faithful to love others through you. In 1 Thessalonians 4:9, Paul told us, "Now about brotherly love we do not need to write to you, for you yourselves have been taught by God to love each other." Who better to teach us how to love than the one who is love?

We can also learn how to become the encouragers God wants us to be by learning from those people the Lord brings into our lives to be teachers and examples. As a matter of fact, we should all be maturing, becoming the examples and teachers ourselves. First Timothy 4:11–12 says, "Command and teach these things ... set an example for the believers in speech, in life, in love, in faith and in purity."

I hope that anytime I get cocky and prideful, thinking I can carry on alone, the Lord will always be faithful to give me a loving lesson—like a prompt squirt in the face. Isn't there a Scripture that tells us that pride goeth before a squirt? I do hope, however, that if it ever happens again, I'll at least miss my hair.

On the contrary, those parts of the body that seem to be weaker are indispensable, and the parts that we think are less honorable we treat with special honor. And the parts that are unpresentable are treated with special modesty, while our presentable parts need no special treatment. But God has combined the members of the body and has given greater honor to the parts that lacked it, so that there should be no division in the body, but that its parts should have equal concern for each other. If one part suffers, every part suffers with it; if one part is honored, every part rejoices with it. Now you are the body of Christ, and each one of you is a part of it.

1 Corinthians 12:22–27

part four

Putting on Our Spiritual Bifocals

*Living Life
Focused on Christ*

chapter sixteen

· · · · ·

In-Your-Face Grace

A few years ago, makeup was something I wore just because I was old enough to get away with it. A hint of color here, a splash of flair there. These days, makeup is a necessity. And it takes time. What used to be a light touch-up has now become more like a major sheetrock repair. Fill this. Putty that. They call it a makeup sponge, but deep down inside, I know it's a trowel!

In my teens I had a tiny makeup bag that would fit in my purse. Today what I call a makeup kit is really a *toolbox*. I have this nagging fear that eventually someone's going to make me get a permit every morning before I can take on the face project.

The gravity of it all (and please excuse the gravity pun) hit me hard one morning when I was blow drying my hair. I was blow drying upside down to get that "big hair" effect that all of us Texas-born women go for, and I inadvertently caught a glimpse of my upside down face in the mirror. It was horrifying—truly one of the more traumatic experiences of my life. It looked like my face was dangling about two inches past my nose! Traumatic, I tell you.

Sharing the Pain

I don't know why I was so disturbed, but I was sure

my girlfriends could help me sort it all out. So I shared my flappy-face trauma with some of my forty*ish* friends at a ladies gathering. Several had similar horror stories to tell. Donna, one of the more positive ones, shouted, "But watch me have a beautiful moment!" Then she sprawled herself on her back on the floor. Her theory was that if you let gravity work for you, the flappy part of the face disappears somewhere into the hairline. Personally, I'm still wondering how you're supposed to actually *hear* someone tell you you're having a beautiful moment when your ears are full of face!

If you haven't yet hit that flappy-faced time of life, we can still be friends, but little of this will make sense to you. In fact, I'll sound like your mother. My only consolation is that eventually, gravity will hit you, too. I say that, of course, in the most sincere Christian love—even if you do hear faint maniacal laughter in the background.

Flapless Grace

What about the Proverbs 31 virtuous woman? Granted, most of us have decided that she may have been Vulcan or an early alien visitation from some other near-perfect race, but Scripture clearly says she smiles at the future. I think it's more than smiling at her real estate and clothing businesses, her fancy garden, or the matching red outfits she's made for her family. She is clothed with strength and honor and kindness. That's what others see.

Have you ever noticed that we never see anything about her physical beauty anywhere in this passage? Did she have a flappy face problem? Who knows? It's more important for us to know that it just didn't matter. Verse 25 says that she "can laugh at the days to come." I guess that's one of the pieces of good news. As the days go by, we have more and more to laugh about.

When we focus on loving and serving him, all the other things fall into place. Well, you know what I mean. You're not going to see your face fall where it used to. But the true beauty of this woman is in her heart. "Charm is deceptive, and beauty is fleeting; but a woman who fears the LORD is to be praised" (Prov. 31:30).

This Semi-old House?

I know our bodies are the temple of the Holy Spirit, and that some of us are feeling like our temples may be in need of some serious repair, but the temple is for worship of our awesome Creator. When we focus on him instead of our bodies, we can smile at the future too, and we can put beauty in its proper perspective.

As for me, I knew for certain that the flappy-face trauma was behind me when I awoke one night thinking someone was lying next to me—and it was ME!

On to the next trauma.

A good woman is hard to find,
and worth far more than diamonds.
Her husband trusts her without reserve,
and never has reason to regret it.
Never spiteful, she treats him generously
all her life long.
She shops around for the best yarns and cottons,
and enjoys knitting and sewing.
She's like a trading ship that sails to faraway places
and brings back exotic surprises.
She's up before dawn, preparing breakfast
for her family and organizing her day.
She looks over a field and buys it,
then, with money she's put aside, plants a garden.

First thing in the morning, she dresses for work,
    rolls up her sleeves, eager to get started.
She senses the worth of her work,
    is in no hurry to call it quits for the day.
She's skilled in the crafts of home and hearth,
    diligent in homemaking.
She's quick to assist anyone in need,
    reaches out to help the poor.
She doesn't worry about her family when it snows;
    their winter clothes are all mended and ready to wear.
She makes her own clothing,
    and dresses in colorful linens and silks.
Her husband is greatly respected
    when he deliberates with the city fathers.
She designs gowns and sells them,
    brings the sweaters she knits to the dress shops.
Her clothes are well-made and elegant,
    and she always faces tomorrow with a smile.
When she speaks she has something worthwhile to say,
    and she always says it kindly.
She keeps an eye on everyone in her household,
    and keeps them all busy and productive.
Her children respect and bless her;
    her husband joins in with words of praise:
"Many women have done wonderful things,
    but you've outclassed them all!"
Charm can mislead and beauty soon fades.
    The woman to be admired and praised
    is the woman who lives in the Fear-of-GOD.
Give her everything she deserves!
    Festoon her life with praises!

                    Proverbs 31:10–31, THE MESSAGE

chapter seventeen

· · · · ·

Such a Spectacle!

Neck-jerk reactions—I've caught myself in several of them recently. Not so many *knee*-jerk reactions, but plenty of the *neck* variety.

I've been noticing my neck-jerk reactions when my five kids come home from school and, as is their usual routine, shove catalog-sized stacks of papers in my face. At first I thought something might be wrong with the copier at school. How did the print get so small and blurry? Then I found that newspapers, books, and magazines all seemed to be using the same copier. Was it some sort of neck-wrenching chiropractic conspiracy?

A few months ago I was doing the daily tug-of-war with my son. "Look at this, Mom!" he said as the paper was plunged toward my nose. He was pushing the paper face-ward. I was struggling to get it to the right reading distance. Me pushing; him pulling. He was winning. I finally crossed my eyes and strained to focus. "Your teacher means for you to wear underwear in a glass curtsy?" I asked, trying to clarify.

After he managed to catch his breath from all the uproarious laughter, he howled, "No, Mom! She wants jelly beans for the end of the year class party!"

Let's See You Laugh at This!

I couldn't think of a good reason to ground him. Disciplining a kid for uproarious laughter didn't seem quite right. But I was thinking that instead of offering merciless laughter, he could've offered to show me the note from the right distance—like the other side of the room. It was all a little exasperating. At least I figured I could call the push and shove routine "resistance training." If nothing else I could chalk up the encounter as my workout for the month. I'm not sure whether to keep the aerobic tug of war in my fitness routine, make an appointment with the ophthalmologist, or head for the chiropractor's office.

The problem, is I've been undeniably nearsighted all my life. But I thought that as I approached the time of life when we tend to get more farsighted, it would offset the nearsightedness and my vision would just get better. It was all part of that "I'm not getting older, I'm getting better" philosophy. I figured what I lost in near-vision I'd make up for in distance. I had no idea I'd lose both! I now have contacts so I can see far away, glasses so I can read when someone shoves papers up my nose, and another pair of glasses so I can see to find my contacts and/or my glasses. Eye chart? What eye chart?

Take a Spiritual Look-see

There's a spiritual visual acuity that's nothing to josh about. Clear focus means the difference between keeping our lives on the right track and totally missing the chart.

Paul addressed it in Philippians 3:13–16 (MSG) when he said, "I've got my eye on the goal, where God is beckoning us onward—to Jesus. I'm off and running, and I'm not turning back. So let's keep focused on that goal, those of us who want everything God has for us. If any of you have something else in mind, something less than total commitment, God will clear your blurred vision—you'll see it yet! Now that we're on the right track, let's stay on it."

Got anything else in mind? Blurred vision is caused by a spiritual eye that's focusing on self, on success, on money—on anything other than Christ. Paul also instructed us to focus on the things of Christ in Colossians 3:1–2 (MSG): "So if you're serious about living this new resurrection life with Christ, *act* like it. Pursue the things over which Christ presides. Don't shuffle along, eyes to the ground, absorbed with the things right in front of you. Look up, and be alert to what is going on around Christ—that's where the action is. See things from *his* perspective." If we want to see things from his perspective, we need to look up and to focus our whole attention on Jesus.

Is This Better, Or Is This Better?

There's a spiritual eye ailment we might call "pressed-by-self-opia." It's a result of thinking we have to make things happen on our own, in our own strength. Trying to take control of our future and straining toward a worldly idea of achievement is like squinting in a room with no light.

"My-oh-my-opia" is another spiritual sight problem. It's worrying and fretting over our future instead of trusting the God who holds it in his hands. Then there's the one we might call "no-clue-opia." It's a shortsightedness regarding the true power of God, being clueless regarding what really matters in life—and who is in control.

Our spiritual vision problems can be corrected when we look at all these issues through the corrective lens of God's Word. Get an up-close and personal look and see for yourself!

Don't Be Shortsighted

The best kind of sight is "insight." Insight comes when we're learning to see things from his perspective. There is great wisdom in staying focused on Christ and keeping our eyeballs zeroed in on him and on his Word. There's no better, more fulfilling way to live. Catch the vision. No bifocals required.

Is it better to focus on my way or his? I can answer that one with my eyes closed! Seeing clearly to respond to his calling is what makes life rewarding and gloriously sweet. Focus on Christ and you'll see life in an entirely new and exciting light. It can add unspeakable joy to your life—and a 20/20-twinkle in your eye!

I ask—ask the God of our Master, Jesus Christ, the God of glory—to make you intelligent and discerning in knowing him personally, your eyes focused and clear, so that you can see exactly what it is he is calling you to do, grasp the immensity of this glorious way of life he has for Christians, oh, the utter extravagance of his work in us who trust him— endless energy, boundless strength!

Ephesians 1:17–19, THE MESSAGE

chapter eighteen
· · · · ·
Mirror, Mirror

I had another one of those "terror-in-the-mirror" experiences the other day. It was early in the morning when I crowbarred myself out of bed. I groggily headed to the bathroom, but when I got there, I was jolted awake when I caught a glance of an absurdly alarming sight in the mirror. I FOUND SOMEONE ELSE LOOKING BACK AT ME! Can you imagine? Talk about a frightening encounter!

Who's the Scariest of Them All?

Mirror, mirror on the wall—who was that woman? She was chubbier than me—probably a little shorter, too. And she certainly had more laugh lines than I do. (What in the world had been so funny to this gal?) Her hair was standing up all over her head in a none-too-attractive, willy-nilly style. I thought for a minute she might be trying for an Einstein kind of look. Or maybe it was one of the characters on *Sesame Street*. Either way, the look was *not* working for her. She didn't look nearly as smart as Einstein or even remotely as cute as Elmo.

I hesitate to even mention a little residual makeup from the day before that she must've missed when she scrubbed her face. I couldn't help but notice that none of her leftovers were where she should have left them. Was that an extra eye on her forehead or just some vagrant mascara that had traveled north? New Age statement or traveling makeup residue—either way it was disturbing. I felt like she was staring at me with all three eyes.

But those pillow marks were probably the most unsettling of all. The lady must have been lying on a couple of giant pillow wrinkles that cloned Frankenstein-looking ruts all across one cheek. *That's going to leave a mark,* I thought. It looked like a couple of those marks were the kind that last well into the afternoon. I'm just so glad that never happens to me.

The part that really fooled me was that she was wearing *my* jammies and robe, but, with as much humility as I can muster, I must say that they really do look much better on me. My jammies, my robe, yet a vague, messed-up resemblance of the rest of me. I couldn't imagine who was behind such an elaborate prank! Imagine changing the entire reflection in the mirror!

Reflect on This

Here's something better to reflect on. As children of God, we are called to be reflections of his glory. As I look into the mirror of my spiritual life, I have to ask myself on a regular basis exactly what kind of image I'm reflecting.

If I'm walking in the Spirit and living in his love, focusing fully on Christ, then it's a loving spirit of grace and glory that others will see reflecting from my life. I'll reflect his image. And here's good news: If there's changing to be done in the spiritual look of that image in the mirror, I'm tickled to say that I serve a God who is faithful to make all the right changes. He's transforming me into his image. That's the perfect look! Second Corinthians 3:18 (NKJV) says, "But we all with unveiled face, beholding as in a mirror the glory of the Lord, are being transformed into the same image from glory to glory, just as by the Spirit of the Lord." Transformed by the very Spirit of the Lord so that I can reflect his glory!

Get a New Image

Colossians 3 tells us how we have taken off the old self with its spiritual pillow marks, makeup leftovers, and crazy hair. We've taken off everything spiritually ugly and put on the new self "which is being renewed in knowledge in the image of its Creator" (v. 10). Romans 6:6–8 tells us that the old ugly self died with Jesus even before we were born, so that we can have the freedom to live a life focused on Christ—we can choose to say no to sin and that old way. "For we know that our old self was crucified with him so that the body of sin might be done away with, that we should no longer be slaves to sin—because anyone who has died has been freed from sin. Now if we died with Christ, we believe that we will also live with him."

Ephesians 4:22–24 says, "You were taught, with regard to your former way of life, to put off your old self, which is being corrupted by its deceitful desires; to be made new in the attitude of your minds; and to put on the new self, created to be like God in true righteousness and holiness." Being made new in the attitudes of our minds and putting on the new self is better than getting rid of mascara residue. It leads to righteousness and holiness—the kind only the Lord can create in our lives.

It's All about Image

These days it's all about image. I want mine to be, well, *his*. *The Message* puts 2 Corinthians 3:18 this way: "And so we are transfigured much like the Messiah, our lives gradually becoming brighter and more beautiful as God enters our lives and we become like him."

Brighter and more beautiful? Someone should probably tell that scary woman I saw in the mirror that she doesn't need to worry about physical beauty. Becoming brighter and more beautiful is really about how much we're allowing the Father to work in our lives— whether or not we're looking like him, reflecting his perfect look. We need to make it our goal, the focus of our lives, to be able to "behold as in a mirror the glory of the Lord."

I guess that takes a lot of the pressure off that pitiful gal in the mirror. I suppose I'll be the one to tell the poor thing that she doesn't need to worry if she's not exactly "the fairest of them all." I have this funny feeling I'll be seeing her again.

But we have this treasure in jars of clay to show that this all-surpassing power is from God and not from us. We are hard pressed on every side, but not crushed; perplexed, but not in despair; persecuted, but not abandoned; struck down, but not destroyed. We always carry around in our body the death of Jesus, so that the life of Jesus may also be revealed in our body.

Therefore we do not lose heart. Though outwardly we are wasting away, yet inwardly we are being renewed day by day. For our light and momentary troubles are achieving for us an eternal glory that far outweighs them all. So we fix our eyes not on what is seen, but on what is unseen. For what is seen is temporary, but what is unseen is eternal.

2 Corinthians 4:7–10, 16–18

chapter nineteen
. . . . .
Wake Up and Smell the Jerky

accidentally made a new discovery. I left the coffeepot on all day, and when I checked it before bedtime, an entire pot of coffee had been reduced to a layer of tar in the bottom of the pot. It was black and sort of chewy-looking. I sniffed it, just out of curiosity, and I think it gave me a little bit of a caffeine buzz.

That's when it hit me that I might really have something. What if I peeled it off the bottom of the pot and cut it into strips? Voila! Coffee jerky! Just think what this could mean to all those heavy-eyed weekday commuters. Instead of testing their spirituality by sloshing scalding coffee in their laps and all over their nice leather seats, they could just pop out a hunk of coffee jerky for a test-free, stain-free commute. I'm thinking it would be a great way to make a pot of coffee last all day, too. It would take several hours just to get it all out of your molars. Residual caffeine!

Caffeinating the Community

Coffee jerky could be just the jolt needed, not only for the commuters, but for scores of those poor individuals fighting off morning comas. What about skyscraper construction workers? Think about the bomb squad workforce. And how about the downtown window washers? Any job not conducive to dozing off—or juggling a thermos, for that matter—would be the perfect jerky job. Roofers, for instance, would be great candidates for lugging around a pocketful or two of java jerky, don't you think?

There's a thought. Not only would the coffee jerky solve the thermos-juggling problem for a roofer, but if he happened to run out of tar, he might even consider plunking down a few strips of jerky—instant roof! Hmm, I wonder what would come out of the drain spouts in the first post-jerky-tar rain. I can almost hear the weatherman predicting clouds with scattered java showers throughout the day.

We could rid our society of certain problems associated with marathon board meetings, lengthy descriptions of new equipment from the tech guy—even eight o'clock classes with monotone professors. I can almost hear the instructor. As soon as a student's eyes started to cross, he could simply throw out the "How do you take your jerky?" question. Not only could we stop the dozing before the eye-crosses and jerk-nods, but we could virtually eliminate desk drool pools for our posterity. This discovery could raise the national average on standardized tests! I'm telling you, there are far-reaching applications and implications to this jerky deal. We might actually be able to help keep our entire society more alert!

Stay Perky

Alertness is a good thing. First Peter 5:8 instructs us to "Be self-controlled and alert," and then tells us why: "Your enemy the devil prowls around like a roaring lion looking for someone to devour." Creepy, isn't it? It would terrify us if we didn't have the rest of Scripture to tell us that our heavenly Father is infinitely more powerful than the Enemy. We even have the next verse in the passage to charge us to "Resist him, standing firm in the faith" (v. 9).

There's also powerful instruction in verse 7: "Cast all your anxiety on him [God] because he cares for you." You can do the resisting, the standing, and the casting all while completely decaf. That's because all of it—from the toughest worries to the simplest tests—all of it falls on the one who takes care of anything and everything through the deep love and infinite care he has for you. What an amazing blessing—we can toss all worries, stresses, and anxieties on him and rest in knowing, as sure as college kids sip cappuccino, he'll take care of it perfectly.

Of course, casting all your anxiety on Jesus doesn't mean you have to slip into a vegetative state. There's no place for a spiritual coma in the work of Christ. In java jargon, we need to "stay perky." "Self-controlled and alert," remember? It's so utterly remarkable that when we surrender our troubles to him that we are truly freed to be focused and alert to a Christ-centered life, focusing on the things in life that really count with an espresso kind of charge. It's better than anything caffeinated, yet it won't keep you up at night. As a matter of fact, giving your anxieties over to Jesus and focusing your life on him is exactly what you need for a peaceful night's sleep. Put that in your pot and perk it!

First Thessalonians 5:4–8 says, "But you, brothers, are not in darkness so that this day should surprise you like a thief. You are all sons of the light and sons of the day. We do not belong to the night or to the darkness. So then, let us not be like others, who are asleep, but let us be alert and self-controlled. For those who sleep, sleep at night, and those who get drunk, get drunk at night. But since we belong to the day, let us be self-controlled, putting on faith and love as a breast-plate, and the hope of salvation as a helmet."

So don't fall asleep—stay alert, focused, and self-controlled in Christ, with or without the jerky. I might encourage you, though, to keep an eye on anything you leave perking in your coffeepot. I think the stage right after coffee jerky is coffee *ash*. Not FDA approved. Not pretty, either.

Keep a cool head. Stay alert. The Devil is poised to pounce, and would like nothing better than to catch you napping. Keep your guard up ... It won't be long before this generous God who has great plans for us in Christ—eternal and glorious plans they are!—will have you put together and on your feet for good. He gets the last word; yes, he does.

1 Peter 5:8–11, THE MESSAGE

chapter twenty
· · · · ·
Clicking for Love in All the Wrong Places

I have to admit, I'm a bit of a Web-maniac. I was reading a book the other day (the bound, paper kind), and I caught myself trying to scroll to the next page. Where do you click these things? I guess it was worse the time I had to write a magazine article without my computer, and I couldn't remember how to do a manual spell check. No one has ever really been able to adequately explain to me how you can look up a word in the dictionary to find out how to spell it when you have to know how to spell it to look it up.

Still, I've heard that there are folks out there who are much more computer obsessed than I am. They're constantly caught trying to defrag their digital clocks and find a better screen saver for their microwaves. I hate to even mention the computer heads who've forgotten how to introduce themselves without asking, "What's your html?"

Are You a Computer Potato?

You might be among the computer obsessed if you've discovered you can't let a TV commercial pass without checking your email. If you can turn your keyboard upside down and shake out enough food crumbs for a seven-course meal, I'd say you're dangerously close to Web-obsession.

If mousework persistently wins out over housework, or if you realize you haven't left the house since the last big sale at Best Buy, you just might be a compulsive clicker. When your only muscles are in your fingers, or when you find yourself heading for bed (finally) and you tell your spouse that your screen saver is about to kick in, it's probably time to consider letting a friend do an intervention.

Be Ready to Unplug

No matter what stage of Web-compulsion we're experiencing, it's always good to remember that it's easy to "get beached" surfing the Net. There are sneaky sites and snakey hooligans lurking, waiting to pounce.

The sites are not only luring men, though the porn sites aimed at them are too numerous to count. But there are also millions of women who have the wrong idea of romance and unrealistic views of an attentive love. There are women who've been hurt or disillusioned who become easy prey to the Enemy's schemes. The Enemy loves to convince women that there's more romance available than they're experiencing and that it's okay to become emotionally connected to men they're not married to. Women are falling into email infidelity every day. Some, convinced that no one will ever know, find themselves searching for the wrong kind of love in all the wrong places and in all the wrong kinds of ways. They're getting snagged by the masses. Sin is such a sly trap.

The result has been deception of singles, disrupted and broken marriages and families, and disillusioned, disenchanted people who end up emptier than ever. In the last chapter, we looked at 1 Peter where we're instructed to "Be self-controlled and alert. Your enemy the devil prowls around like a roaring lion looking for someone to devour. Resist him, standing firm in the faith, because you know that your brothers throughout the world are undergoing the same kind of sufferings" (1 Peter 5:8–9). Let's not be fooled. That Enemy is on the prowl on the Internet, too, and he's devouring those who are lacking in self-control and who haven't stayed alert.

We need to be ready to unplug—to run, even sprint, from the worldly things that seek to pull us down. Second Timothy 2:22 in *The Living Bible* urges us to "Run from anything that gives you the evil thoughts." There is safety and life when we learn to run from evil influences and run to Christ. Proverbs 16:17 says, "The highway of the upright avoids evil; he who guards his way guards his life."

Taking the Right Turns on the Information Highway

There are wonderful opportunities and amazing facts, truths, and tidbits of information available to us as a result of our entrance into the Computer Age. The information highway has proven to be a powerful tool for sharing God's Word and for exponentially increasing the number of people we can reach, teach, and encourage. We simply need to make sure we stay on the upright road on this information highway and make sure we use our computer power for good and not evil. One translation puts Proverbs 16:17 (CEV) this way: "God's people avoid evil ways, and they protect themselves by watching where they go." We can avoid evil and protect ourselves by watching where we go in life, and by watching where we go on the net. Attentive love comes from God. He's the one who gives the ability to give and receive the right kind of love in all the right ways. We're blessed when we learn to love and to respect others and to love and to honor the Lord with everything we are and with everything we have. We need to make sure the time we spend (and the *amount* of time we spend) on the computer is God-honoring. Our focus should always be on him. And if we get to the place where we realize we've never seen any of our best friends' faces, it might be time to rethink the intervention idea.

Everything in the world is about to be wrapped up, so take nothing for granted. Stay wide-awake in prayer. Most of all, love each other as if your life depended on it. Love makes up for practically anything. Be quick to give a meal to the hungry, a bed to the homeless—cheerfully. Be generous with the different things God gave you, passing them around so all get in on it: if words, let it be God's words; if help, let it be God's hearty help. That way, God's bright presence will be evident in everything through Jesus, and he'll get all the credit as the One mighty in everything—encores to the end of time. Oh, yes!

1 Peter 4:7–11, THE MESSAGE

part five

Surrendering Control in a Control-top World

*Choosing
Obedience to God*

chapter twenty-one
· · · · ·
Living a Superwoman Life in an Olive Oyl Body

I went to visit a friend who had just had a baby. She had just given birth and she was wearing *jeans*. Little, tiny, size 6 jeans! And she looked really spectacular in them. *Pul-lease!* It was a disturbing sight to behold.

I asked her if she could at least put on a baggy top so the rest of us wouldn't have to look at that. After all, I was in those baggy blouses six months postpartum. As a matter of fact, I'm still in some of those tops and I'm *ten years* postpartum. Yet there she was, in those teeny jeans three days after giving birth. It just seemed wrong.

Tough to Stomach

If you want to talk about disturbing sights in the other direction, I'll tell you about giving birth to my five babies. Five *large* babies. I didn't really want to discuss stomach muscles (or the lack thereof) with my flat-stomached, teeny jeans friend, but let's just say that I don't think even Superwoman could hold in this belly. After the third or fourth baby, I was pretty much gathering the stomach somewhere near the knees, rolling it up (sort of like putting away the kids' slip-and-slide) and tucking it in the top of my industrial-strength, control-top pantyhose. If you got a load of my stomach only, you might very well mistake me for an invertebrate.

Life in the Super City

Living here in "Flabsville" is not exactly like life in Metropolis, but I decided I probably like it better than the alternative: working off the flab. I'm convinced some of it is just not going. It's found a comfy home, it's rather happy here, and it's just not leaving. But five-baby flab on Olive Oyl muscle tone? Ms. Universe I'm not.

I tried a version of the "get out of Flabsville" alternative anyway with some fitness training. You've already heard me whine about how that turned out, right? My "training" turned out to be more of a "train" *wreck.* At least the flashbacks have started to subside.

Then I tried something near an all-spinach diet. One of my eyes started to close in Popeye fashion after about the second week of over-spinaching myself. I didn't even seem to be "stronger" to the finich when I ate me spinach. Getting whipped into shape really is a job for Superwoman!

It's a Bird, It's a Plane . . .

Where does *real* strength come from? Our all-powerful God, the one who made the universe with less than a wink, has strength ready and waiting for the asking. It's not the Popeye/Superwoman kind of muscle. No, even better. He offers us the strength to live this life exactly as it was meant to be lived. Real muscle!

Isaiah 40:28–31 says, "Do you not know? Have you not heard? The LORD is the everlasting God, the Creator of the ends of the earth. He will not grow tired or weary, and his understanding no one can fathom. He gives strength to the weary and increases the power of the weak. Even youths grow tired and weary, and young men stumble and fall; but those who hope in the LORD will renew their strength. They will soar on wings like eagles; they will run and not grow weary, they will walk and not be faint." Strength for the weary and power for the weak? It's spinach and anti-Kryptonite all rolled into one!

And he doesn't just give the strength to do a few things. He gives any kind of strength we'll ever need to do anything that we really need to do. Philippians 4:13 says it perfectly: "I can do everything through him who gives me strength." He gives strength to do most things? Some things? No. Everything!

How to Escape the Wimpy Life

How do we get that kind of strength? Surrender! We exercise our trust muscles by trusting Christ in complete and radical obedience. It's the kind of training that will never end up in a train wreck. As a matter of fact, the more reps you do, the easier it becomes to trust again the next time.

It's all about learning to trust the Lord instead of trusting self. Trusting self leads to the wimpy life—a life full of fear, doubt, and the agony of defeat. No strength. That's what happens when we're in control. It's even more futile than expecting the control-top pantyhose to control a five-baby belly roll.

Spinach-free Strength

As we give control to the one who has the only real and ultimate strength, faster than a speeding bullet we find the kind of strength we've needed all along. If you're wanting to pump up, try a study of the strong armor of God in Ephesians 6:10–13. It says, "Finally, be strong in the Lord and in his mighty power. Put on the full armor of God so that you can take your stand against the devil's schemes. For our struggle is not against flesh and blood, but against the rulers, against the authorities, against the powers of this dark world and against the spiritual forces of evil in the heavenly realms. Therefore put on the full armor of God, so that when the day of evil comes, you may be able to stand your ground, and after you have done everything, to stand." Check out each piece of the armor in verses 14–17: belt of truth, breatplate of righteousness, shoes of peace, shield of faith, helmet of salvation, and the sword of the Spirit. He's got us covered!

There is unspeakable strength in his mighty armor. Surrender control and give his armor a try. You'll find total strength, eternal muscle. Never mind the spinach.

My counsel for you is simple and straightforward: Just go ahead with what you've been given. You received Christ Jesus, the Master; now live him. ... You're well constructed upon him. You know your way around the faith. Now do what you've been taught. School's out; quit studying the subject and start living it! And let your living spill over into thanksgiving. ... You don't need a telescope, a microscope, or a horoscope to realize the fullness of Christ, and the emptiness of the universe without him. When you come to him, that fullness comes together for you, too. His power extends over everything.

Colossians 2:6–7, 9–10, THE MESSAGE

chapter twenty-two
Calendar-itis

My dentist's office called last week to tell me that I missed the appointment I didn't know I had. How embarrassing. The problem was that I lost my calendar for an entire week. Life stopped until it was recovered.

My calendar contains most of my brain cells. Without it, I might accidentally deliver Daniel to ballet and Allie to the fourth grade boys' basketball practice. Or what if I accidentally delivered Daniel to one of my speaking engagements instead? Can you picture him blinking dazedly from the podium of a women's conference? And what about the orthodontist appointments? With five kids and sixty-plus ill-fitting molars, missing the Rhea appointments might leave a black hole in the orthodontist's schedule that could suck the office datebook right into next year. Could that cause some sort of breach in the space/time continuum? It could at least result in one whirlwind of a month!

We're Not in Kansas Anymore

Since losing my calendar was so like losing my brain, I ended up bouncing from place to place in Scarecrow fashion trying to find anyone who had even a clue where the rogue planner might be. It was like a bad Oz scene. I was singing "If I Only Had a Brain" at every stop. My head definitely had that "full of stuffin'" feeling. My calendar doesn't exactly "unravel any riddle for every individ'le," but it does generally help keep the individ'les heading to the right appointments, obligations, and social events.

The reason it's such a tragedy to misplace that brain-thing is because it's so completely crammed full of those events: meetings, kids' guitar and art lessons, writing deadlines, speaking dates—a leatherbound tornado waiting to touch down. The twister threat caused a case of calendar-itis that lasted the entire week.

Just What the Doctor Ordered

When I finally found the stray calendar, I really had to give it a pretty serious analysis. Okay, first I did the "found the calendar" happy dance of joy. But after that, I knew it was time to take a look at the schedule. Any time losing a datebook causes extreme calendar-itis—and slight hyperventilation—it's time to seek treatment. Treatment for me consists of a thorough examination of the schedule and prompt surgical removal of unnecessary obligations, followed by daily application of affected area (calendar) to a prescribed altar—Christ's.

Before we plan our days, we need to remember that our heavenly Father has plans for us. In Jeremiah 29:11 (NCV) he said, "I know what I am planning for you. ... I have good plans for you, not plans to hurt you. I will give you hope and a good future."

A Calendar with Purpose

In *The Purpose Driven® Life,* Rick Warren comments on what adopting Christ's purposes for your life can do for your schedule:

Knowing your purpose simplifies your life. It

defines what you do and what you don't do. Your purpose becomes the standard you use to evaluate which activities are essential and which aren't. You simply ask, "Does this activity help me fulfill one of God's purposes for my life?"

Without a clear purpose you have no foundation on which you base decisions, allocate your time, and use your resources. You will tend to make choices based on circumstances, pressures, and your mood at that moment. People who don't know their purpose try to do too much—and that causes stress, fatigue, and conflict.

It is impossible to do everything people want you to do. You have just enough time to do God's will. If you can't get it all done, it means you're trying to do more than God intended for you to do.[1]

Choosing the Right Road

Everyone is asking how to stop the madness. How do we find that unhurried life? How do we stop tapping on the steering wheel, wishing people would drive faster? How do we enjoy that time in line, rather than mentally listing all the things we could be doing instead? How do we enjoy conversation with our kids without wishing they would hurry up and get to the point?

Somewhere along the road, I've had to come to the conclusion that I'm not Wonder Woman. That shouldn't have been a tough conclusion to reach, right? But since I'm not Wonder Woman, I just can't do it all. None of us can. That means we have to use the wisdom God gives us to make choices.

We make wise choices when we learn to stay in tune with the spiritual gifts God has given us. We get a good hint as to where those gifts lie when we examine our lives and see where God is using us.

We're also better equipped to make those choices when we've invested time in studying the wisdom we find in his Word. We're better equipped when we've spent time with the Lord in prayer. Tough to do when the schedule gets hairy, I know. But it's essential in those busy times if we want our life to be about the kingdom and not just about the hubbub of a full calendar.

As we spend time with him, we find ourselves more in tune with what his will is for our calendar. Pray about a busy day. You may find yourself blocking out some of the less important activities when the Lord brings someone to your heart and mind that you need to encourage. You just never know what might happen when you put your calendar on his altar, but I can tell you this: Whatever happens will be so much more peace-inducing than scrambling to merely check things off of a busy to-do list.

Follow the Yellow-Brick Road?

Dorothy had to choose a direction on her yellow-brick journey. The Scarecrow gave her some pretty brainless counsel: "Of course, people do go both ways." It reminds me of how I can end up meeting myself coming and going when my calendar is out of whack. But that's the straw-headed road. There's no peace there. There is, however, great peace in heading down his road of true purpose. Isaiah 26:3 (TEV) says, "You, LORD, give perfect peace to those who keep their purpose firm and put their trust in you."

Every now and then, we need to pull off the road, yellow-bricked or not, and think about the Father's plans for us. Take some time to ponder his plans for you. Who knows? You might think of things you never thunk before!

People with their minds set on you, you keep completely whole, steady on their feet, because they keep at it and don't quit. Depend on GOD *and keep at it because in the* LORD GOD *you have a sure thing. Those who lived high and mighty he knocked off their high horse. He used the city built on the hill as fill for the marshes. All the exploited and outcast peoples built their lives on the reclaimed land. The path of right-living people is level. The Leveler evens the road for the right-living.*

Isaiah 26:3–7, THE MESSAGE

chapter twenty-three
· · · · ·
Drop and Give Him All

Do I have to admit how many things I've started and never finished? I was doing some cleaning the other day and found a cross-stitch project I started for my baby's room. The baby is now seventeen. I found some fabric, too, and that was troubling. Not only can't I remember why I bought it, I can't remember buying it. I don't even sew. If I were in a military school focused on project-finishing, I think there would be grounds for a court martial.

Since I'm already branded, I guess I'll go ahead and confess the handful of half-read books on my shelf and the dozens of half-articles floating inside my computer.

Still, probably one of my most distressing not-quite-finished projects was one from a couple of years back. I was in a meeting with a publisher, and I glanced down to notice my nine polished nails. I had gotten distracted mid-polish and missed a nail! I was supposed to convince this editor that I could responsibly write an entire book, but I couldn't even manage to paint all ten nails? If I were in project boot camp, this would probably be when the drill sergeant would shout, "Drop and give me twenty!" Or in the case of my nails, at least all ten!

Marching Orders

Discipline in every part of our spiritual lives is important. How successful and fruitful can we be as Christians if we can't make ourselves do the things we're supposed to do?

At least we're in good company in the struggle. Paul said in Romans 7:15–16 (MSG), "What I don't understand about myself is that I decide one way, but then I act another, doing things I absolutely despise. So if I can't be trusted to figure out what is best for myself and then do it, it becomes obvious that God's command is necessary."

You bet God's command is necessary—if it was necessary for Paul, how much more for us! *Discipline* is following Christ as his *disciple* with a "Sir, yes, Sir!" If we want a life filled with meaning—eternal meaning—then we need to let the Father pour his kind of discipline into our lives, marching in good order down the disciplined road. Proverbs 10:17 (MSG) tells us that "the road to life is a disciplined life."

Still, Paul got downright frustrated with himself. He so wanted to do the right thing but found himself doing wrong. That's when he asked, "Is there no one who can do anything for me? Isn't that the real question?" Then he gave us the answer: "The answer, thank God, is that Jesus Christ can and does. He acted to set things right in this life of contradictions where I want to serve God with all my heart and mind, but am pulled by the influence of sin to do something totally different" (Rom. 7:24–25 MSG).

Grace-ipline

A well-adjusted life balances discipline with grace. There are going to be times when we mess up. There is grace. And we don't need to feel as if we're being bullied into obedience by God, our Drill Sergeant. Ephesians

3:20 (MSG) says, "God can do anything, you know—far more than you could ever imagine or guess or request in your wildest dreams! He does it not by pushing us around but by working within us, his Spirit deeply and gently within us."

It's not a bullying on his part, but an invitation on our part—an invitation to come in and take control and to give us the strength to live the way we were meant to. It's a strengthening by his Spirit— "not a brute strength but a glorious inner strength—that Christ will live in you as you open the door and invite him in" (v. 16–17 MSG).

Strength through Weakness

"Whipping ourselves into shape" isn't really the answer either. Real strength comes when we understand our weaknesses, just as Paul did in 2 Corinthians 12. In verse 9 (MSG) the Lord said to him, "My grace is enough; it's all you need. My strength comes into its own in your weakness."

I'm pretty excited that strength comes through weakness—that means that I have a lot to work with! There's a lot of weakness here, even if you don't bother doing a nail polish inventory. Isaiah 40:29 (NKJV) says, "He gives power to the weak, and to those who have no might He increases strength." What great news!

Philippians 2:12–13 (MSG) tells me that God is the one who is working in me, giving me desire to obey him, giving me the power to do what I need to do to please him. "Be energetic in your life of salvation, reverent and sensitive before God. That energy is *God's* energy, an energy deep within you, God himself willing and working at what will give him the most pleasure." There's no greater joy than the joy we find in doing what we were created to do, to give him pleasure.

"For the Purpose of Godliness"

So many undisciplined and frustrated soldier-wanna-bes are struggling to find the disciplined life just so they can feel better about themselves. But if we're struggling to become disciplined for our own satisfaction, we're operating from selfish motives. How can godliness be accomplished without selflessness?

Godliness should be my underlying purpose in the first place. First Timothy 4:7 (NASB) says, "Discipline yourself for the purpose of godliness." I guess that means that I need to, in essence, put myself in God's boot camp. Drop and give him *all*. The 1 Timothy passage continues: "For physical training is of some value, but godliness has value for all things, holding promise for both the present life and the life to come" (v. 8).

Pleasing the Commander

I want to be a disciplined soldier in this present life. Second Timothy 2:4 says, "No one serving as a soldier gets involved in civilian affairs—he wants to please his commanding officer." There's a worthy goal: To please him consistently. That's what I want to aim for—I want to be a good soldier. I'd even like to be the kind of soldier who manages to paint all ten nails.

But what happens when we live God's way? He brings gifts into our lives, much the same way that fruit appears in an orchard—things like affection for others, exuberance about life, serenity. We develop a willingness to stick with things, a sense of compassion in the heart, and a conviction that a basic holiness permeates things and people. We find ourselves involved in loyal commitments, not needing to force our way in life, able to marshal and direct our energies wisely.

Galatians 5:22–23, The Message

chapter twenty-four

· · · · ·

More than Meets the Nose

A friend walked into my house the other day and said, "Mmm, I love the smell of broccoli cooking." That was nice. Except I don't like the smell of broccoli. And except for the fact that I wasn't cooking broccoli.

Here's the cooking tip of the day: If you receive the broccoli comment when you're making vanilla pudding, something is very, very wrong.

We had stale granola bars for dessert.

Foraging for Pudding

A few days later I actually did make broccoli. I guess my friend's broccoli comment reminded me that there is such a thing as edible greenery. The fact that I'd forgotten sort of guilted me into buying some. My kids don't like much of anything green except mint chocolate chip ice cream and lime Airheads. When they hear the word "salad," they associate it with grazing. They will eat green vegetables when I can manage to herd them in that direction, though I wouldn't put it past a couple of them to call a social worker to report child abuse of the taste buds if I tried to make green stuff on any kind of a regular basis.

I knew no one in the family would eat enough of the

broccoli to really get much out of it, but I made it anyway so I would be providing something healthy for my children *not* to eat. I can't really explain the logic. Maybe it's just in case the nominations are still open for Mother of the Year and there's a hidden camera in my kitchen.

Of course, if there's a hidden camera in my kitchen, the award is definitely out anyway. Don't the judges frown on an "all paper, all the time" dinnerware policy, a refrigerator that contains old containers of furry macaroni and cheese, and soup with more skin than vegetables, not to mention an appliance garage that frequently parks dirty dishes instead of blenders and toasters?

Anyway, I was just glad the broccoli didn't smell like pudding. Of course, it never smelled quite like broccoli, either. And it kept making my eyes water. I'm sorry to say, stale granola bars didn't make a great vegetable. At least they're high in fiber—and they rarely make you tear up.

Nosing Around the Heart

I don't mean to sound "nosy," but if people could sort of "sniff" our spirits, do you think they could they tell what we're really made of? One of our life goals should be for all those around us catch a giant whiff of love whenever we're near. We learn that kind of love from God the Father—and it perfumes our lives and makes living so very sweet. Ephesians 5:1–2 says, "Be imitators of God, therefore, as dearly loved children and live a life of love, just as Christ loved us and gave himself up for us as a fragrant offering and sacrifice to God."

Did that say "fragrant" offering? Here's where it all starts to make "scents." Jesus loves us so much that he gave his life—his *all*—on our behalf. Now there's a love we can sink our olfactory nerves into! It's amazing to think that when our Father gives us a heavenly sniff, he breathes in the fragrant offering of Christ. His amazing love is even more than meets the nose!

Get a Whiff of This

As we breathe in the Father and learn to imitate him, we learn to really live a life of love. Learning to imitate him means learning to be surrendered to what he wants for our lives and becoming lovingly obedient to what he wants us to do. He's told us in no uncertain terms that loving others is even more tightly wrapped to obedience than smell is to broccoli. We're told in 2 John that it's not a new command, but one we've had from the beginning: "I ask that we love one another" (2 John 1:5). The next verse says, "And this is love: that we walk in obedience to his commands. As you have heard from the beginning, his command is that you walk in love" (v. 6).

Walking in Love

I want my life to be a fragrant offering as I learn to obediently walk in his commands. Isn't it wonderful that through that obedience we learn to walk in love—real love. I love that! I love it a gajillion times more than vanilla pudding—even with chocolate sprinkles.

As for the Mother of the Year award, I'm letting that go. I've decided not to get my "nose out of joint" over it, either. With support and cheers from my children, I'm moving toward less broccoli, more pudding. I'm using chocolate-related reasoning: Pudding has milk, milk has calcium, calcium is healthy. Therefore, pudding is health food. I think I can make it work if I toss out a salad for them to graze on now and then. When I told the kids about our health food diet, they voted me the Mother of the Year in the Rhea house. I don't think I've been this proud since the boys demonstrated to me that they could burp John 3:16. Doesn't it just make a mama tear up?

Admittedly, even when I do chuck the greenery and opt for making pudding, there are no guarantees it won't still smell like vegetation. There's no guarantee that it won't make me tear up, either—and I'm not talking about tears of pride and joy. That's why I've also decided to try to make sure I at least keep a fresher box of granola bars on hand.

Let grace, mercy, and peace be with us in truth and love from God the Father and from Jesus Christ, Son of the Father!

I can't tell you how happy I am to learn that many members of your congregation are diligent in living out the Truth, exactly as commanded by the Father. But permit me a reminder, friends, and this is not a new commandment but simply a repetition of our original and basic charter: that we love each other. Love means following his commandments, and his unifying commandment is that you conduct your lives in love. This is the first thing you heard, and nothing has changed.

2 John 1:3–7, The Message

chapter twenty-five
Cut and Dry

It's confession time. I've done a terrible thing. The logical part of me kept warning me not to do it, but I just couldn't make myself listen. I did it anyway. *I cut my own bangs.* Every time I take the scissors into my own hands, I promise myself I'll never do it again. That's because every time I take the scissors into my own hands, I end up looking at little like Mr. Spock, minus the ears. This, however, is no way to live long and prosper.

Hair 911

When am I going to get it? I'm just not a skilled bang-cutter. When I try, I'm operating miles outside my area of expertise. And this kind of operation is usually near fatal for the patient. Somebody get a crash cart. I need some serious hair CPR.

The gal who cuts my hair, on the other hand, does a great job. Rhonda (yes, she and I have the same first name) knows what she's doing around a pair of hair-cutting scissors. She can trim, gel, clip, and mousse with the best of them.

She's so good, as a matter of fact, that her calendar is crazy. So is mine. But whenever we're having a hard time getting our schedules together, all I have to do is call her up and say in a menacing voice, "I'm holding the scissors to my head." It's sort of a hair suicide threat. Then she'll say, "Okay, okay, okay! Just *don't cut your own bangs!*" She'll usually finish up with, "Now put down the scissors and slowly step away!"

She's pretty adamant about me staying away from hair self-service. She knows whatever mess I make—and I *will* make a mess—she'll have to straighten out. Picture me in her chair whining, "Rho-o-o-nda, can you fix this, plea-ea-ease?"

Do-It-Myself? I Don't Think So!

Isn't it strange that I would take the scissors into my own hands again, knowing my past haircutting record? I've thought about it, and I don't care how badly I needed an operation, I'm quite sure I would never snatch the scalpel from the surgeon's hand with an, "Oh, let me do that! I saw an appendectomy on the Health Channel one time. I can do this!"

In an eternal perspective, I guess my hair—even my appendix—is not as important as it may seem. As a matter of fact, hair and body parts are simple compared to running a life. Yet how many times have I snatched the controls on that, too?

Doesn't it make more sense to leave the life-controlling to the expert? You know, the one who designed the life in the first place? When I'm really stylin' is when my all is on the altar and I'm leaving the reigns in my heavenly Father's capable and loving hands.

When I take control of my own life, I make a mess every time. I'm operating miles outside my area of expertise. I end up limping back to God with a whiney, "Lo-o-ord, can you fix this, plea-ea-ease?" Wouldn't it be easier to simply be obedient in the first place?

The "Shear" Facts

According to the experts, over half of Americans believe it's more important to please God than to be successful, yet most of us don't have a clue what that means. And would you believe almost a third have "enjoyment" as the goal and purpose for life? So most of us want to please God, but really don't know exactly what that means or how to do it.

We please God and show our love for him by surrendering the scissors, so to speak, in complete obedience. Jesus said in John 14:15 (MSG), "If you love me, show it by doing what I've told you."

Obedience Brings Joy

In John 15:10–11 (MSG), Jesus told us that real enjoyment—the goal and purpose for life for so many people—actually comes from pleasing God, from keeping his commands: "If you keep my commands, you'll remain intimately at home in my love. ... I've told you these things for a purpose: that my joy might be your joy, and your joy wholly mature."

Joy and fulfillment don't need to become such a "hairy" deal. Our joy becomes "wholly mature" when we're putting first things first and living our lives in obedience. That obedience can feel as sweet and comfy as Home Sweet Home when we remain intimately at home in the love of the Lord. How sweet to be at home in his love!

No one says it better or more plainly than Jesus: "The person who knows my commandments and keeps them, that's who loves me. And the person who loves me will be loved by my Father, and I will love him and make myself plain to him" (John 14:21 MSG). There's really no place like home.

Serious Obedience

Jesus doesn't beat around the bush regarding our obedience. He told us in Matthew 7:21 (MSG) that "serious obedience" is what's required: "Knowing the correct password—saying 'Master, Master,' for instance—isn't going to get you anywhere with me. What is required is serious obedience—*doing* what my Father wills."

Understanding that the "Father controls best," and that we should respect his area of expertise generates satisfaction and a life with an outcome that affects those around us. According to Proverbs 10:27, "The fear of the LORD adds length to life, but the years of the wicked are cut short."

Did it have to say "cut short"? Just another reminder that I'm spending the next couple of weeks suffering severe bang humiliation.

"Whoever has my commands and obeys them, he is the one who loves me. He who loves me will be loved by my Father, and I too will love him and show myself to him."

Then Judas (not Judas Iscariot) said, "But, Lord, why do you intend to show yourself to us and not to the world?"

Jesus replied, "If anyone loves me, he will obey my teaching. My Father will love him, and we will come to him and make our home with him. He who does not love me will not obey my teaching. These words you hear are not my own; they belong to the Father who sent me."

John 14:21–24

part six

Maid to Order

*Serving God
with a Whole Heart*

chapter twenty-six
. . . . .
I'm a Little Teapot

I've heard that house dust is made up of 97 percent skin cells. Isn't that thoroughly fascinating and utterly disgusting all at the same time? Here's the good news. I think I'm collecting enough to build myself a MAID! Right now she's under my refrigerator. Do you suppose I can train her to do laundry, clean windows, and serve high tea?

I do love a good cup of tea. I come from a long line of tea drinkers. From early in life I knew how to enjoy a nice pot of tea. I even liked the "I'm a Little Teapot" song. I liked the song, that is, until I got a little older and started *looking* more like a teapot. Singing happily about how I'm "short and stout"? I don't think so.

On the Other Hand-le

There is a version, though, that my husband taught me that has always cracked me up. I still sing this one. Maybe you've heard it, too; it goes like this:

"I'm a little teapot, short and stout.
Here is my handle,
Here is my handle—
Hey, I'm a sugar bowl!"
(Don't you just love a surprise ending?)

Shaped to Serve

It makes me think of how God crafted and shaped us to be exactly who we are. He didn't get to the finished project and say, "Oh no! I was trying for a teapot on this one!"

There's big-time frustration in trying to be something or someone God has not designed us to be. It's like a teapot trying to be a sugar bowl—or a vacuum cleaner—or a B-52! It's just not going to work. But as the teapot surrenders to the purpose its designer had in mind, do you know what happens? The teapot is filled up with goodness and warmth. Then, as it serves, it shares that warmth and goodness with others. It's doing exactly what it was made to do. What could be more satisfying for a teapot?

Pouring Ourselves Out

Paul said in Ephesians 4:1–3 (MSG), "In light of all this, here's what I want you to do. While I'm locked up here, a prisoner for the Master, I want you to get out there and walk—better yet, run!—on the road God called you to travel. I don't want any of you sitting around on your hands. I don't want anyone strolling off, down some path that goes nowhere. And mark that you do this with humility and discipline—not in fits and starts, but steadily, pouring yourselves out for each other in acts of love, alert at noticing differences and quick at mending fences."

Excuse me, did Paul tell us to be steadily *pouring ourselves out?* Well, tip me over!

Spilling Out Love

We pour ourselves out for each other in "acts of love." How it must please our heavenly Father when we're sacrificing ourselves in order to pour love into others. That's service with a smile, just as we're taught in Galatians 5:13–14: "You, my brothers, were called to be free. But do not use your freedom to indulge the sinful nature; rather, serve one another in love. The entire law is summed up in a single command: 'Love your neighbor as yourself.'"

Not only does it please the Lord: We're taught plainly that when we're pouring our lives into others and serving them selflessly, we're not only serving others, we're obediently serving the Lord. And that's just how we should see it. Ephesians 6:7 says to "Serve wholeheartedly, as if you were serving the Lord, not men."

Second Corinthians 9:12–15 encourages us. It tells us that our service can even morph into thanks to God, into praise to him, and into prayer to him. Isn't that a magnificent thought? "This service that you perform is not only supplying the needs of God's people but is also overflowing in many expressions of thanks to God. Because of the service by which you have proved yourselves, men will praise God for the obedience that accompanies your confession of the gospel of Christ, and for your generosity in sharing with them and with everyone else. And in their prayers for you their hearts will go out to you, because of the surpassing grace God has given you. Thanks be to God for his indescribable gift!"

That kind of loving service calls for humility. It's pride that causes us to look at someone else's gifts and abilities and think that we should be called to serve in the same way. In 1 Corinthians 12:4 we read that "There are different kinds of gifts, but the same Spirit." The Lord is the one who has divvied out the gifts by his grace. He's the one we should desire to serve—and in whatever capacity he desires us to serve.

Getting All Steamed Up

So maybe a good prayer for us to pray is *Lord, fill us up with you—then tip us over and pour us out! Use us to serve in every big way and every small way—in any way you desire. Use us to serve in every way that will bring glory and honor to you!*

Serving his way answers the searching questions about your purpose in life—whether you're called to be a teapot or a vacuum cleaner! And the Lord is the one who can provide the most joyful "surprise ending."

Since we're talking about the searching questions, can I admit that I did have one more deep question? If I asked my under-the-fridge maid to dust the furniture, would I be causing her to wipe out an entire future generation?

It is absolutely clear that God has called you to a free life. Just make sure that you don't use this freedom as an excuse to do whatever you want to do and destroy your freedom. Rather, use your freedom to serve one another in love; that's how freedom grows. For everything we know about God's Word is summed up in a single sentence: Love others as you love yourself. That's an act of true freedom. If you bite and ravage each other, watch out—in no time at all you will be annihilating each other, and where will your precious freedom be then? My counsel is this: Live freely, animated and motivated by God's Spirit. Then you won't feed the compulsions of selfishness.

Galatians 5:13–16, THE MESSAGE

chapter twenty-seven
. . . . .
Choose This Day

I went to buy some face cream the other day and found the store was out of my usual brand. I thought it should be easy enough to pick a different one—there were tons of them to choose from. But all the rows of choices created a new problem. I saw some with eucalyptus, wheat germ, and wild honey. Others had almonds and mint. Was I supposed to put this stuff on my face or make a casserole? I read the label on one and was almost sure that it read the same as the marinade I use for chicken. On the other hand, my chicken really is pretty tender. This could work. But I was sure I needed just the right combo.

Which to choose, which to choose? Did I want anti-aging or wrinkle-fighting? (Shouldn't I have both?) Did I want daytime or nighttime formula? (I guess I would need to decide at what time of day I would rather shrivel up.) Should I choose aloe or Vitamin E? Cream or lotion? Paper or plastic?

Routine Decisions

The face routine is full of decisions. I remember when I was a teenager, someone asked me which one makeup item would be the toughest to give up. I really had to think. My mascara? My cute, fruity lipgloss? At least that decision is easier these days. Hands down, the one cosmetic item I can't do without now is my *tweezers*. But then, we all know that's another chapter, don't we!

All of life is full of choices. I'm writing this chapter around election time. I think most of us look toward elections as stirring times of hope, change, new commitments to serve, and all the excitement a new slate of elected officials includes. Most of us look forward to those things. But I feel sure that *all* of us look forward to seeing the political ads end! Somebody stop the insanity!

Hmm, now that I think about it, "Somebody stop the insanity!" might make a good campaign slogan. I might consider voting for a person who would contemplate running on a "Just Say No to Psychosis" platform.

Each year during this season, though, I'm reminded that every election day we make another set of choices. Vote for him? How about her? This party or that? He's strong on this issue, but a little wimpy on that one. Sometimes it's confusing. And it rarely produces smoother, more supple skin. As a matter of fact, it can even cause those painfully bothersome worry lines in some folks—usually the people involved in the campaigning, bless their hearts. Did anyone else notice it's called "cam-PAIN-ing"? Still, despite the pain and the major wrinkle potential, we celebrate the fact that we get to choose. What a wonderful privilege and awesome responsibility.

We need to be responsible citizens, even when we don't wholeheartedly support the people in office. God's Word instructs us to "Be a good citizen. All governments are under God. Insofar as there is peace and order, it's God's order. So live responsibly as a citizen. If you're irresponsible to the state, then you're irresponsible with God, and God will hold you responsible.

Duly constituted authorities are only a threat if you're trying to get by with something. Decent citizens should have nothing to fear. Do you want to be on good terms with the government? Be a responsible citizen and you'll get on just fine, the government working to your advantage" (Rom. 13:1–4 MSG).

Choosy Christians Choose Service

Even in our spiritual lives, God has granted us the amazing privilege of choice. Will we serve him? Will we serve worldly objectives? Will we serve ourselves? Joshua 24:15 says, "But if serving the LORD seems undesirable to you, then choose for yourselves this day whom you will serve, whether the gods your forefathers served beyond the River, or the gods of the Amorites, in whose land you are living. But as for me and my household, we will serve the LORD."

The choice is ours. Let's not blow it. Let's roll up our sleeves. Let's make wise choices regarding who serves in government leadership. Let's be even more cautious how we choose who gets our heart service. Deuteronomy 13:4 says, "It is the LORD your God you must follow, and him you must revere. Keep his commands and obey him; serve him and hold fast to him." *The Message* phrases verses 3 and 4 like this: "GOD, your God, is testing you to find out if you totally love him with everything you have in you. You are to follow only GOD, your God, hold him in deep reverence, keep his commandments, listen obediently to what he says, serve him—hold on to him for dear life!"

Joshua gave the people the choice whether to serve worldliness of the past, sinful desires of the present, or the God of all time. The people were free to choose, but "not deciding" was not an option. To choose any way other than God's way was to choose self. It's the same for us.

Will We Serve?

Joshua made the right choice. He chose to serve the Lord. As a matter of fact, he chose wisely for his entire household. I want to make wise choices as well—in all the big areas and in the small ones, too. I want to make a clear stand for Christ and to serve him in a Deuteronomy 10:12–13 (MSG) kind of way: "So now Israel, what do you think GOD expects from you? Just this: Live in his presence in holy reverence, follow the road he sets out for you, love him, serve GOD, your God, with everything you have in you, obey the commandments and regulations of GOD that I'm commanding you today—live a good life."

Thankfully, he allows me to serve, wrinkles and all. As for my face cream, I ended up choosing a drum of the anti-aging, wrinkle-blasting, aloe and Vitamin E-fortified, 24-hour, long-lasting, creamy lotion in a gel formula with added mint, almonds, wheat germ, and a couple of additional marinading ingredients that might also go together to make a nice salad in a pinch. The concoction has worked so well that, alas, now I think I might be too young to vote.

And now, O Israel, what does the LORD your God ask of you but to fear the LORD your God, to walk in all his ways, to love him, to serve the LORD your God with all your heart and with all your soul, and to observe the LORD's commands and decrees that I am giving you today for your own good? To the LORD your God belong the heavens, even the highest heavens, the earth and everything in it. Yet the LORD set his affection on your forefathers and loved them, and he chose you, their descendants, above all the nations, as it is today.

Deuteronomy 10:12–15

chapter twenty-eight

· · · · ·

Tweeze the Day

Since we already brought up the tweeze situation, I might as well ask the question: Remember when we only had to tweeze our eyebrows? These days I start at the chin and work my way up. By the time I make it all the way up to my brows, all the blood has drained out of my arms. Some days I wish I could just give in to brow fur. Other days I find myself wishing brow fur was the only fuzz problem draining the blood from my arms. It seems like I woke up one morning and found some sort of pelt across my upper lip. Who left that there? I didn't know whether I should tweeze it, wax it, or try to train it.

Heel, Boy

I tossed out the training idea and decided I'd go the tweeze route. That's when I found out I was the one who needed the training. Do you know how much stamina it takes to endure a marathon tweeze?

At least I'm seizing the opportunity to increase my writing output. Let's just say that since I've been regularly involved in the tweeze-athons, I've seen my keyboard speed increase exponentially. It's a little embarrassing that my finger muscles are bigger than my biceps.

Carpe Diem

Speaking of seizing opportunities, Carolyn Arends wrote a song awhile back about seizing every opportunity to serve. It's called "Seize the Day." I've been working on a depilatory-type version, incidentally, called "Tweeze Today." Okay, it's not quite as deep and motivational as Carolyn's, but I'll give you the first verse anyway:

I know a girl who tried using a razor
Soon a five o'clock shadow, it hardly could faze her
She's adjusting quite well, since finding new purpose
She's loving her job in the traveling circus

Here's the chorus:

Tweeze today, tweeze whenever you can
Or next thing you know you will look like a man
Tweeze today, hey—keep tweezers at hand
To keep any stray fur at bay
Tweeze today

Did it bring a tear to your eye too? There's something especially moving about the inspirational challenge to stay on top of every tweeze situation—blue arms or no blue arms.

Never Give Up!

Just as Carolyn Arends' song inspires, I want to be even more tenacious about staying on top of my service for Christ. She writes,

Seize the day, seize whatever you can
'Cause life slips away just like hourglass sand
Seize the day, pray for grace from God's hand
Then nothing will stand in your way
Seize the day

And I love the last verse:

Well one thing I've noticed, wherever I wander
Everyone's got a dream he can follow or squander
You can do what you will with the days you are given
I'm trying to spend mine on the business of living[1]

What's one of the secrets to making the most of life? Understanding that it's the "grace from God's hand" that makes life count. It's easy to get weary in the everyday hassles of ministering to imperfect people in an imperfect world. Let's not give in to weariness! Galatians 6:9 says, "Let us not become weary in doing good, for at the proper time we will reap a harvest if we do not give up."

Knowing we're keeping our passion for doing the works the Lord has called us to do can be energizing even in itself. We're doing what we were created to do! Romans 12:11 instructs us to "never be lacking in zeal, but keep your spiritual fervor, serving the Lord."

Know When to Make a Pit Stop

Granted, keeping our spirits on fire for Christ sometimes involves knowing when it's time to take a little rest. Our bodies require rest, and we can serve him better when we give our bodies what they need. As a matter of fact, we can even serve him in our resting—it can help us stay pluckier than ever. (Did I really use the word "pluckier" in the tweeze chapter?)

Romans 12:11–12 in *The Message* says this: "Don't burn out; keep yourselves fueled and aflame. Be alert servants of the Master, cheerfully expectant."

Staying fueled and aflame makes for an exciting life in Christ and can save us from the perils of burnout and fruitlessness. How sad it would be to have a life "squandered." Keeping the excitement in the Lord can help us make the most of every opportunity. Ephesians

5:15–16 (MSG) says, "So watch your step. Use your head. Make the most of every chance you get."

Making the Most

I'm trying to be more discerning with how I use my time these days. Do you think it would be a waste of time to work on another tweeze-type song? Since I couldn't think of a word that rhymes with "electrolysis," I was thinking of doing a pelt version instead called, "Fleas Astray."

Hey, maybe I could go in a totally new direction with a cryogenics version called "Freeze Today." Or maybe a version for parents with students entering college called "Fees to Pay." How about a song for allergy sufferers: "Sneeze Away."

Nah, on second thought, I think if I try another one, I'll just stick to the most direct and the most fruitful version: "Please Obey."

Don't be misled: No one makes a fool of God. What a person plants, he will harvest. The person who plants selfishness, ignoring the needs of others—ignoring God!—harvests a crop of weeds. All he'll have to show for his life is weeds! But the one who plants in response to God, letting God's Spirit do the growth work in him, harvests a crop of real life, eternal life. So let's not allow ourselves to get fatigued doing good. At the right time we will harvest a good crop if we don't give up, or quit. Right now, therefore, every time we get the chance, let us work for the benefit of all, starting with the people closest to us in the community of faith.

Galatians 6:7–10, THE MESSAGE

chapter twenty-nine
· · · · ·
Runners in the Stockings of Life

On the average, men and women get ready on a whole different clock. Men usually have a squirt of water they call a shower. For women, on the other hand, if it's not a 35-minute drain of the hot water tank, we almost surely have parts left undone. Guys shave one face—maybe. We women can beat that with one armpit tied behind our backs (though that sounds incredibly uncomfortable). Then we still have to take on a makeup job we could fairly accurately compare to overhauling an engine—and sometimes it takes around the same amount of time.

The guys wrap up by getting dressed. That's it. They just get dressed. Women don't merely get dressed. Women *accessorize*. And that happens only after deciding that whatever outfit they originally chose would probably look better with that other white blouse. Then it's decided that the white blouse looks best with the other blue skirt, which means, of course, the shoes also have to go. Most of the time the only shoes that really will go are the ones at the mall. Those mall trips have been known to significantly slow down the readying process.

Cream Filling

The woman's readying journey is filled with assorted creamy chemicals—elements and compounds for every step of the journey. Lotions, moisturizers, spritzes—a special concoction for every part. The lard-filled cream goes on the face, hair cream (in gel, mousse, WD40, and every other consistency) goes into the 30-minute hair-do development. Then there's the all-over body cream, the under-eye cream, cream depilatories, cream perfumes—you name it, we cream it.

Guys get ready. Women get creamed. Creaming takes longer.

Getting Ready on the Run

Why is it that when we're getting ready, no matter how much time we have left, we need at least twenty minutes more? And have you ever noticed that the days when you're twenty minutes behind the "twenty-minutes-too-little" schedule, those are the days you discover a monstrous run in your only good pair of pantyhose?

Our spiritual lives can hit the same kind of snags. We have so much we'd like to accomplish for the Lord. We see things moving along at a good clip in our service for Christ when, RIP!—a major runner-like interruption. It may be a difficult physical situation or a troubling financial challenge. It might be a heartache. It might even be an attack from a godless person who would like nothing better than to see you knuckle under in the conflict.

The Tough Keep Running

I want to be a "runner" no matter what. No, not that kind of runner. I want to be the kind of runner who doesn't wimp out of the race when the going gets tough, persevering in service for the Lord, serving despite adversity.

Will there be difficult times—snags in this life? Oh yes. God's Word tells us to expect them, so don't let them catch you off guard. First Peter 4:12–13, 19 says, "Dear friends, do not be surprised at the painful trial you are suffering, as though something strange were happening to you. But rejoice that you participate in the sufferings of Christ, so that you may be overjoyed when his glory is revealed. ... So then, those who suffer according to God's will should commit themselves to their faithful Creator and continue to do good."

We're told to "continue to do good"—keep on serving! The Lord didn't ask us to serve only when life is easy. He just asked us to serve. And keep on serving. Hebrews 6:10–12 (MSG) tells us that God notices when we keep on serving: "He knows perfectly well all the love you've shown him by helping needy Christians, and that you keep at it. And now I want each of you to extend that same intensity toward a full-bodied hope, and keep at it till the finish. Don't drag your feet. Be like those who stay the course with committed faith and then get everything promised to them." We're called to "keep at it" with intensity.

Joy in the Snags

Not only does the Lord notice our perseverance when difficulties come along, but on top of it all, he even uses those very difficulties to build more perseverance and maturity. "Consider it pure joy, my brothers, whenever you face trials of many kinds, because you know that the testing of your faith develops perseverance. Perseverance must finish its work so that you

may be mature and complete, not lacking anything"
(James 1:2–4).

Consider it pure joy? It can happen when we see
those runners in the stockings of life as opportunities
to experience the tiniest taste of the sufferings of
Christ and to let those sufferings produce in our lives
the character qualities we need to acquire to become
"mature and complete, not lacking anything."
Maturity brings joy. *The Message* calls it a gift:
"Consider it a sheer gift, friends, when tests and chal-
lenges come at you from all sides. You know that
under pressure, your faith-life is forced into the open
and shows its true colors. So don't try to get out anything prematurely. Let it do its work so you become
mature and well-developed, not deficient in any way"
(James 1:2–4).

There's a revelation waiting for us at that place of
maturity. It can be such a surprise to find that life
doesn't have to be snag-free to be joyful. The snags can
be fruitful wrinkles in life's journey. Don't worry,
they're the kind of wrinkles that don't necessarily
require cream.

*Don't be naïve. There are difficult times ahead. As the end
approaches, people are going to be self-absorbed, money-
hungry, self-promoting, stuck-up, profane, contemptuous of
parents, crude, coarse, dog-eat-dog, unbending, slanderers,
impulsively wild, savage, cynical, treacherous, ruthless,
bloated windbags, addicted to lust, and allergic to God.
They'll make a show of religion, but behind the scenes
they're animals. Stay clear of these people.*

2 Timothy 3:1–5, THE MESSAGE

chapter thirty
· · · · ·
Taking the Plunge

We have a toilet in one of our bathrooms that has a notoriously sticky handle. I'm forever sending kids back to jiggle. It can be a real nuisance. We also have a toilet that tends to overflow now and then. There's an intermittent, ongoing plunge need that can get pretty bothersome, too. I never realized how the two little nuisances could become such a crisis of cataclysmic proportions when they're both in the same toilet. I put the calamity equation together pretty quickly, though, once I was in the middle of the ugliest overflow situation I've ever seen.

I wish I could say I quickly sprang into action. But after I heard the screams of disgust from a couple of my kids, I ran to the bathroom door. Then I froze. I just stood there for several seconds, staring in horror at the toilet-volcano that was erupting toxic lava all over the bathroom. Is this what happens when disaster victims go into shock? It didn't help that I was wearing pantyhose—and no shoes. I fought off the shock effects and struggled to be daring and heroic. No time to hunt shoes, it was a "plunge in" kind of situation.

Tiptoe through the Marshmallows

I tiptoed in, took the top off the tank, and at least stopped the eruption part, but I was so grossed out that I wasn't quite sure what to do next. I opened up the cabinet to see which towels I could live without (forever), and when I pulled the door open, six rolls of toilet paper came tumbling out. Within a few seconds the six rolls poofed to the size of twelve. I felt like I was stepping through a minefield of giant marshmallows. *Oh well,* I thought, *at least they're absorbent.*

I found a new respect and appreciation for the shop vac that day. And I can't tell you how glad I am that maintenance of any item with the word "shop" in it (if it's the kind that's not related to the mall) falls under my husband's jurisdiction.

Needless to say, I threw away the toilet paper. I threw away the towels, too. And the pantyhose. Also the rug, shower curtain, and the kids' toothbrushes— just for good measure. I would've thrown away the shop vac, too, but Richie wouldn't let me. As much as I appreciate it, I never want to see that thing again.

By the third or fourth shower I started to feel better.

Let Your Ministry Overflow

Sometimes flushing out just the right place to serve the Lord can seem almost as tricky. Thankfully, it's not nearly so messy. But it may require a "plunge-in" attitude. Not diving in because another person tells us to, or because we feel guilty if we don't, and not diving in without thought, but sensibly diving into service because that's what God has called us to do. God's Word gives us "plunge in" instructions in 2 Timothy 1:7 (MSG): "God doesn't want us to be shy with his gifts, but bold and loving and sensible." And verse one of chapter two charges us, "So, my son, throw yourself into this work for Christ."

Whatever our situation, one thing is clear: We're supposed to be serving. First Peter 4:10 says, "Each one should use whatever gift he has received to serve others, faithfully administering God's grace in its various forms." Not one of us is left out of the charge. Each one has received a gift. Each one needs to be using that gift in service for Christ.

Paul instructed Timothy in chapter four of 1 Timothy to keep on using his special gift of ministry. Paul told him to "keep that [gift] dusted off and in use" (v. 14 MSG). Then he said to "Cultivate these things. Immerse yourself in them. The people will all see you mature right before their eyes! Keep a firm grasp on both your character and your teaching. Don't be diverted. Just keep at it. Both you and those who hear you will experience salvation" (vv.15–16 MSG).

Believe me, when he says to "immerse yourself," it's nothing like the toilet situation at my place. You can count on a better experience—and one that will result in your maturity, right out there for everyone to see.

The Head Hunter

Are you looking for a job? Have you been searching for your ministry? Check in with the heavenly Head Hunter. The best place to start a search for a place of ministry is on your face. Pray for direction. Pray for fruitfulness. Pray for courage. Pray to be used by God to make a difference in his kingdom, no matter how big or how small the job. Those are just the kind of prayers he wants to answer.

Sometimes finding your ministry is as simple as looking at what God has gifted you to do. Sometimes it's as simple as asking yourself where your passions in ministry lie. What gets you revved up? Is there an area of service you feel the Lord has placed on your heart?

Discovering your place of service often involves trying some new things and searching out those gifts God wants you to use. Go ahead. Step out of your comfort zone. You might be surprised to find yourself in a new, rewarding ministry, overflowing in fruit and satisfaction. Overflowing in the best way—without the shop vac.

So, my son, throw yourself into this work for Christ. Pass on what you heard from me—the whole congregation saying Amen!—to reliable leaders who are competent to teach others. When the going gets rough, take it on the chin with the rest of us, the way Jesus did. A soldier on duty doesn't get caught up in making deals at the marketplace. He concentrates on carrying out orders. An athlete who refuses to play by the rules will never get anywhere. It's the diligent farmer who gets the produce. Think it over. God will make it all plain.

2 Timothy 2:1–7, The Message

part seven

Grace To Go

Sharing Christ
in a Needy World

chapter thirty-one
. . . . .
True Grit

There's nothing quite like a family vacation to the beach. Surf, sun, and sunscreen have a way of drawing a family closer. I can usually even get past the bathing suit part, though there's definitely an annual swimsuit trauma that results in the entire family eating menus centered around celery for four weeks. (In a perfect world, eating chocolate would turn cellulite into muscle) My family endures "Annual Celery Month" because they love the beach payoff (even if they don't love my celery and rice-cake casserole).

We came home from our last beach trip with a ton of souvenirs. Actually, it was a few souvenirs and a ton of *sand*. A beach vacation truly is a close family time, but the traveling involves a different kind of closeness—elbow-to-elbow in the car. It's even more uncomfortable on the way home when there's sand between each elbow.

Spreading Beach Cheer

We still seem to be inventorying bushels of souvenir sand. I think we have more now than we had then. Does this stuff multiply? It seemed at every rest stop on the way home, we could open the car door and see yet another pile of sand pour out. We left little "dunes" across six states. There was sand in each shoe, sand in every suitcase, sand in each pocket—all times seven people! It doesn't even wash out of the clothes, it just sort of moves around.

I have to admit there came a time when I wanted absolutely nothing more to do with our souvenir sand. I could hardly close my mouth without feeling grit scritching between my teeth. I really have to draw the line at souvenirs in my molars.

The good news is that we don't have to save up for any more of those beach vacations. Not because we didn't enjoy the beach, but because I think we brought most of it home with us. From now on, I can just blow up a couple of beach balls and send the kids to the car.

I still had to be careful unpacking. I had to keep an eyeball on the cat at all times. When he noticed suitcases full of sand, he thought we had brought souvenirs home for him! It was a litter/grit disaster just waiting to happen.

Scritch on This

Have you ever thought about the grit of salt? To be honest, I never thought much about its grittiness. I guess it's because I so enjoy what it can do to a bag of fries—even a celery casserole. But what if the salt weren't, well ... salty? Without its saltiness, it would merely be an annoying scritch between the molars.

In Matthew 5:13, 16, Jesus said, "You are the salt of the earth. But if the salt loses its saltiness, how can it be made salty again? It is no longer good for anything, except to be thrown out and trampled by men. ... let your light shine before men, that they may see your good deeds and praise your Father in heaven."

Salt seasons. It has a purifying effect. It makes people thirsty. It's even used to preserve. Without our saltiness, we're just grit. We're like the sand without the fun of the beach.

I should never take a vacation from asking myself the big "salt" questions:

- Am I spicing up life for those around me?
- Am I having a purifying effect on the people I meet?
- Am I encouraging others to thirst for Jesus?
- Am I allowing God to use me to preserve life, or am I ignoring the spiritual death in those I encounter every day?
- Am I allowing the Lord to use my saltiness to show off his good works and bring glory to him, or am I just empty grit?

The Nitty-gritty Dirt on Salt

Physically, our body salt is measured in our blood, sweat, and tears (it's more than just another rock group).

Tears—Our tears can help measure our saltiness spiritually, too. What do we treasure enough to cry about? Our tears can be invested in friends and family. They can show our remorse over our sin. Tears are incredibly precious to our Father.

Sweat—Sometimes our saltiness for Christ is measured by how much we're willing to sweat for him. First Corinthians 15:58 says, "Always give yourselves fully to the work of the Lord, because you know that your labor in the Lord is not in vain."

Blood—There are places in our world where being salt for Jesus results in the ultimate sacrifice; people are called to bleed. Maybe the biggest salt questions should be: Am I willing to sacrifice myself if it means my heavenly Father will be glorified? Can I abandon all, knowing I belong to the Lord?

I want to be salt—not just grit. Mark 9:50 says, "Have salt in yourselves, and be at peace with each other." That's our salty charge!

I get a little charge/reminder every time I pull out my favorite vacation shorts and stick my hands in the pockets. You guessed it. It's a mini-trip to Grit City.

If your hand causes you to sin, cut it off. It is better for you to enter life maimed than with two hands to go into hell, where the fire never goes out. And if your foot causes you to sin, cut it off. It is better for you to enter life crippled than to have two feet and be thrown into hell. And if your eye causes you to sin, pluck it out. It is better for you to enter the kingdom of God with one eye than to have two eyes and be thrown into hell, where "their worm does not die, and the fire is not quenched." Everyone will be salted with fire.

Salt is good, but if it loses its saltiness, how can you make it salty again? Have salt in yourselves, and be at peace with each other.

Mark 9:43–50

chapter thirty-two
· · · · ·
Shoe-mania

It's always exciting to move into a new home. Don't you just love having everything all nice and spanking clean? Yes, it's great—that is, until you move all your not-so-spanking stuff in. That's when you find out what a clutter nut you really are. I noticed during our last move that the clutter revelation was even more apparent when making a move from a massive master bedroom closet to a normal one. I discovered I'm not only a clutter nut, I'm a bona fide shoe maniac.

Colorwheel of Shoes

I found black heels, black pumps, black flats, black casuals, black loafers, black boots—even black tennies. And those were just the black ones. There were equally impressive numbers in every other color. I ran across shoes in greens, purples, blues, reds ... and who knew there were so many different shades of tan? I found shoes in hues and styles without even an outfit to match. It was bizarre. I even found lonely, mateless shoes! Why was I keeping those? Can you picture me stylin' in a one-shoe look? It's tough to convey that fresh-off-the-runway appearance hopping on one foot.

With that visual, I made myself get rid of the mateless shoes. Progress. But there were still tons more.

There were leathers, vinyls, plastics, fabrics—every natural and man-made shoe material you could think of—animal, vegetable, mineral! How in the world was I supposed to cram all these shoes into my new petite-sized closet?

My husband suggested getting rid of some of them. That was, of course, crazy talk.

You Gotta Have Shoes

Shoes are important. Shoe authorities say we need good shoes—many of us spend a good portion of our day on our feet. They say having a good foundation helps keep us up and running.

Me? I mostly just want to look good. Shoes are a foundational part of a fashion statement. They complete a look. Don't you just love it when you're sporting a new pair and someone notices? Knowing your feet look gorgeous—now that's satisfying!

Our Spiritual Shoes

God's Word teaches us the importance of our spiritual shoes. I think we could call it the "soul" of our shoes, couldn't we? Whatever we call it, I want my spiritual shoes to get noticed in a whole different way.

Beautiful feet to our Father are the feet of those who carry the Good News: Isaiah 52:7 says, "How beautiful on the mountains are the feet of those who bring good news, who proclaim peace, who bring good tidings, who proclaim salvation."

The Good News is that we can have peace with God through the salvation provided in Christ. These are "good tidings"—it's news of joy! Sharing that joy with others multiplies our own peace and joy. It's a biblical way to reproduce satisfaction in life—and it deepens our own satisfaction to boot! (Did I say "boot"?) Sharing the Good News is more satisfying than a bargain pair of shoes. Eternally more satisfying—even more comfy!

Jesus' Beautiful Feet

Our Savior is the supreme example of beautiful feet. His feet walked this earth to provide the Good News. It's interesting that his feet became their most beautiful as they were mistreated—pierced. It was his piercing that made the final payment on our salvation—and it gave us something incredible to tell. It's a privilege to tell it. So let's get our own shoes on and hit the road, sharing with those who don't know that they can have the same astonishing peace we've been given.

If you're leaving out the "sharing Christ" part of your spiritual life, you're missing something special in your walk with him. It might make your walk a little like a one-shoed hop—off-balance. Sharing the Good News is foundational for completing our spiritual look. It keeps us "up and running."

That's why I've decided to concentrate more on my spiritual look and maybe (gulp) get rid of some of my spare shoes. I think I may have enough to start my own business. Oh well, "There's no business like shoe business."

"Foot-notes"

Have you ever asked yourself what kind of shoe you might be? Take a look at these. Any fits?

- Sneakers—Sneakers are those who will tell someone about Jesus, but they don't want anyone they know to hear them. They have to be careful not to get caught.

- Pumps—They rarely offer any information about what Jesus has done in their lives. If you want to know if these folks are believers, you have to pump them for the information.
- Flats—They're not too sharp about keeping an eye out for opportunities to share. Flats aren't very conscientious about keeping their witnessing tools sharp either. They're not too keen on 1 Peter 3:15: "Always be prepared to give an answer to everyone who asks you to give the reason for the hope that you have."
- High heels—"Heels" is too negative a term, so ignore that part, but there are those who feel a little too "high"—too proud—to share Christ. They feel that job should be left for pastors, Sunday school teachers, and other servant folk.
- Loafers—Loafers know they need to share, they have all the tools they need, but they're a little lazy about stepping out of their comfort zone and doing it. Beautiful shoes need to "get to steppin'."
- Slippers—Slippers are those who have started to slip back into that sluggish frame of mind regarding witnessing. If slippers aren't careful, they can quickly become loafers. It's easy to "slip" into.
- Running shoes—Some Christians are runners. They share the Good News of the Gospel with urgency and energy. Have you ever noticed that runners are usually in the best shape physically? They're the healthiest spiritually, too! Ready to put on your running shoes for Jesus?

Therefore put on the full armor of God, so that when the day of evil comes, you may be able to stand your ground, and after you have done everything, to stand. Stand firm then, with the belt of truth buckled around your waist, with the breastplate of righteousness in place, and with your feet fitted with the readiness that comes from the gospel of peace. In addition to all this, take up the shield of faith, with which you can extinguish all the flaming arrows of the evil one. Take the helmet of salvation and the sword of the Spirit, which is the word of God.

Ephesians 6:13–17

chapter thirty-three
The Perfect Gift

I have some sweet friends who never mention their birthdays. They graciously and humbly let birthdays come and go, never wanting anyone to make a fuss. I love and admire those friends. But, hey, they get really piddly presents. They are wonderfully noble and unselfish. I guess this is the part where I have to admit that I have very little in common with them.

Mark Your Calendar

So, please mark my birthday on your calendar. March 20—Rhonda Rhea's birthday—big letters. You might want to also make a significant-sized note next to it to remind yourself to buy a nice gift. I've been known to send out gift lists and make selections at the major department stores. I'm registered at all my favorite spots. At your request, I can also give you the precise number of shopping days left. I figure if I'm going to have to get a year older anyway, I might as well get as much mileage out of it as possible. There's hardly anything that makes you feel like you've gotten mileage out of a birthday like some really nice loot.

Don't worry if you happen to miss the exact date. (Did I mention it's March 20?) In recent years, I've found it difficult to fit all the partying into one day, so I no longer have a mere birthday. I've designated March as my "birthmonth." The celebration begins on the first and I don't let go of it until the thirty-first, although, admittedly, I've been known to still have some residual partying going on through April. I'm wondering if I should make it a "birthquarter."

I told one of my friends the other day that one of my spiritual gifts is the gift of "receiving." I don't think you'll find it listed in Scripture, but there are definite hints. After all, if it weren't for people like me, what would those with the spiritual gift of giving do? Who could they possibly give *to?* See? I fulfill a purpose in the body of Christ.

It probably won't shock you to find out that I'm a ripper. Have you ever seen people *untaping* their gifts? I realize we all have our own ways of doing these things. But by the time the untapers finally get around to that last piece of tape, they've pretty much had to put me in a straightjacket. I've seen the untapers actually *fold the paper!* I can rip open a good dozen gifts in the time they open one. And after I've opened a gift, there is no paper to fold. As a matter of fact, most of the time, anything left of the gift wrap is mere confetti. I feel like I'm creating more "party" as I rip!

The Most Expensive Gift Ever

While we're on the topic of gifts, would you believe that the greatest, most expensive gift ever purchased is often not accepted? If you're one like me who has the gift of receiving, it's almost unimaginable, isn't it!

Jesus Christ set aside his rights as God and put on human skin to live a sinless life and to die to pay for our sin. He bought our salvation with his life. That's an expensive gift—the life of the holy Son of God! And the gift is offered to all. Yet still there are those who are so wrapped up in the temporary things of this world and consumed with controlling their own worldly lives, that they refuse to accept the gift. Sad, don't you think?

Mark This, Too

There's something I'd like for you to remember—even more than I want you to remember my birthday. There are people who need to be reminded about The Gift. They need to come to an understanding of their desperate need to accept it. There are some people who can't even be reminded. They've not yet heard. We have the awesome pleasure of sharing the message of his gift. And not only do we have the pleasure of sharing it, we have the pleasure of living it out for the world to see. Word gets around when we're sharing it and living it. First Thessalonians 1:8 (MSG) says, "The word has gotten around. Your lives are echoing the Master's Word, not only in the provinces but all over the place. The news of your faith in God is out. We don't even have to say anything anymore—*you're* the message!"

The Gift of the Message

The Bible tells us that "Every good and perfect gift is from above, coming down from the Father of the heavenly lights" (James 1:17). Every single gift that's eternally worth giving or receiving is from our loving Father. Ephesians 2:7–8 (MSG) tells us, "Now God has us where he wants us, with all the time in this world and the next to shower grace and kindness upon us in Christ Jesus. Saving is all his idea, and all his work. All we do is trust him enough to let him do it. It's God's gift from start to finish!" How about that for a gift to rip into!

Praise be to the Father of Lights for the Perfect Gift. He fills our lives with meaning, grants us undeserved grace and love, infuses us with joy, and then gives us a charge. For us gals, it's sort of like the ultimate "You go, girl." And his charge places even more unspeakable value in our purpose for living. Not only those precious gifts, but he goes so far as to give us each at least one birthday every year. (Did I mention mine is March 20?)

Jesus, undeterred, went right ahead and gave his charge: "God authorized and commanded me to commission you: Go out and train everyone you meet, far and near, in this way of life, marking them by baptism in the threefold name: Father, Son, and Holy Spirit. Then instruct them in the practice of all I have commanded you. I'll be with you as you do this, day after day after day, right up to the end of the age."
Matthew 28:18–20, THE MESSAGE

chapter thirty-four
To-Go Order

I was zipping through the drive-through window of one of my favorite fast-food stops the other day. (No surprises so far, right?) It took me forever to decide what I wanted. It was one of those little mind battles: healthy (as healthy as fast food gets, anyway) vs. tasty. The taste buds were winning. Besides, the last time I had a salad at that particular fast-food place, the lettuce was brown. Call me picky, but I like my burgers brown and my lettuce green, and never the twain shall switch.

"Jus ... me know ... whe ... you're rea ... to ord ... ." I'm pretty sure that meant I was supposed to let him know when I was ready to order. Between the muffly tones and all the speaker crackles, who could tell? It was either that or he had dominoes and was battling a redheaded Ninja on a motorcycle. Does anyone else have trouble understanding what comes out of those speakers? I sometimes wonder if there's a special language spoken only in fast-food speaker systems. I think it's akin to Martian.

I finally made my decision and placed my order. The score: taste buds, one; brown salad, zilch. Between the speaker crackling and the burger guilt I guess I got distracted. I absentmindedly leaned over to the speaker and added, "I'll have that to go, please."

Would You Like Crow with That?

Okay, that was a little embarrassing after I thought about it. After all, what would be the alternative to a to-go order in a drive-through? Would a non-to-go order mean I would plan on getting my food, then climbing out and eating on the hood of my car before I left the car line? Or maybe I would get out after I paid, prop my elbows on the pick up window, and eat in front of the cashier. At the very least I'd have to order from the drive-through, drive around and park, then go inside the restaurant—bag in hand—and eat my lunch in their dining room. All the choices were just too weird. Did I hear Martian snickering coming from the speaker?

Make That to Go

Sometimes a to-go order is understood, sometimes it bears repeating. We looked at the "to-go order" that Jesus gave in Matthew. Even though I'm mentioning it again, it's still not redundant like my fast-food to-go order. Chapter 28:19–20 says, "Therefore go and make disciples of all nations, baptizing them in the name of the Father and of the Son and of the Holy Spirit, and teaching them to obey everything I have commanded you. And surely I am with you always, to the very end of the age." Jesus didn't mince words when he commanded us to go. He said we should go and make disciples of all nations. He didn't mention Mars, but he does want those who love him to go to every place on this planet.

Sometimes a to-go order is a location thing, as in "all nations." Sometimes it's a movement thing—a command to get up and get going. Abraham was called to go. What did he do? He went! It wasn't the "where" that got him into the Hall of Faith in the book of Hebrews, it was the "how." He went in immediate uncompromising obedience.

To Go Where?

It's almost funny to think about Abraham pulling up stakes and taking off when we're reminded in Hebrews 11 that he didn't even know where in the world he was going! It could've been an expedition to Mars to search for redheaded Ninjas for all he knew.

Check it out; it was one of those Carmen Sandiego things on a gargantuan, supernatural scale: "By faith Abraham, when called to go to a place he would later receive as his inheritance, obeyed and went, even though he did not know where he was going. By faith he made his home in the promised land like a stranger in a foreign country; he lived in tents, as did Isaac and Jacob, who were heirs with him of the same promise. For he was looking forward to the city with foundations, whose architect and builder is God" (vv. 8–10). God called. Abraham "obeyed and went." Obedience first. Questions later. What a great example of faith and obedience.

Blessing in Going

It's good to remember that when we're immediately obedient, there is blessing. Abraham couldn't see the path in front of him, but he knew where he was ultimately headed. He had already made his home in a promised land he hadn't yet seen.

He lived in tents in this life. For the record, that part blows my mind a little. I've been diagnosed with a severe camping allergy. Camping causes profuse whining. Camping in tents equals intense ("in tents") whining. But I don't picture Abraham as a whiner. He kept an eyeball on his future dwelling. He kept his trust and faith in the architect/builder of his permanent, glorious home. Just think about what's happening with Abraham this very minute. His love, obedience, and faith are being rewarded in ways we can't even imagine. Radical obedience equals radical blessing.

So don't just stand there. Go! Share! Reach out! Don't get too distracted by life—where to live, what to wear, what to eat. Throw on something comfy, grab a burger, and get sharing—boldly going where no earthling has gone before!

Better make that burger to go.

After this the Lord appointed seventy-two others and sent them two by two ahead of him to every town and place where he was about to go. He told them, "The harvest is plentiful, but the workers are few. Ask the Lord of the harvest, therefore, to send out workers into his harvest field. Go! I am sending you out like lambs among wolves. ... He who listens to you listens to me; he who rejects you rejects me; but he who rejects me rejects him who sent me." The seventy-two returned with joy and said, "Lord, even the demons submit to us in your name."

Luke 10:1–3, 16–17

chapter thirty-five
· · · · ·
For the Love of Chocolate

I would guess that about 99.9 percent of us women have a shared passion: the love of chocolate. I've noticed that most men "like" chocolate, while most women *need* chocolate. With every new study that comes out plugging the positive attributes of chocolate (and its ability to extend our lives, produce greater mental acuity, and bring about world peace), I have a hundred women who are faithful to clip the articles, forward and re-forward the emails, and copy the book pages by the gajillions (all while just as dependably ignoring the evil studies that talk about fat, calories, and other scandalous negative chocolate associations). If I kept a chocolate file, it would probably take a Ding Dong truck to transport it. And even before all the studies came out touting the healthful mental and physical benefits of chocolate, I already considered it a health food. It's made from cocoa beans. Beans are a protein, right? Protein is essential for good nutrition. I love my high-protein diet.

Then there's milk chocolate. You know we women need to do our part to guard against osteoporosis, right? Isn't milk a great source of calcium? So shouldn't we take our daily dose of milk chocolate along with the rest of our vitamins? If milk chocolate really is good for our bones, then, while I may not have abs of steel, I would venture to say that I do have bones of steel. Maybe titanium.

Choco-snobbery

I have some friends who are confessed chocolate snobs. They enjoy only the finest, high-class chocolates. They like the kind that can only be consumed with one pinky in the air. If it's not posh, it just won't wash. To these gals, if the chocolate doesn't send them into some kind of debt-recovery program, it's hardly worth their time. They associate only with the chocolate elite in the upscale chocolate neighborhoods.

Me? I'm strictly a low-class chocolate operator. Give me a good, cheap, waxy chocolate and I'm totally content. As a matter of fact, you could probably stick a wick in my favorite chocolate, light it up, and not only have a warm and tasty snack, but a pretty decent light source to boot.

There's hardly anything better than a good friend and some semi-good chocolate. It's some of life's sweetest sharing. Granted, many women maintain that there are certain times of the month when chocolate just isn't meant to be shared. Injuries have occurred. I guess it's a reminder we should all have a little discernment—and a *lot* of chocolate.

How to Share the Best Thing in Life

Sharing with others really is good. Sharing the good news of our salvation is the ultimate in good. God's love gift to us was meant to be shared. The best way to share the message of salvation is to first understand that it's the Holy Spirit who changes a person's life. We don't have the capacity to do that—

even if we try bribing the person with chocolate. Real heart changes happen only through the power of God at work in a life. So when we witness to others, we need to remember that it doesn't depend on us. It doesn't matter how "good" you are at sharing the Gospel—or how you may feel that you fumble through it. What matters is what God does with your sharing in the heart of an individual. He's more powerful than your best choice of words. He's more powerful than your biggest mess-ups. Depend on his power.

Go Prayed Up

That's why we should always wrap our witnessing in prayer. Sharing should be the "meat" of a witnessing sandwich—and prayer is the bread. We should pray that the Holy Spirit will have complete influence over every word we say and that we'll have power from him to share simply, plainly, and truthfully. First Timothy 2:4–8 (MSG) says this: "He wants not only us, but *everyone* saved, you know, everyone to get to know the truth *we've* learned: that there's one God and only one, and one Priest-Mediator between God and us—Jesus, who offered himself in exchange for everyone held captive by sin, to set them all free. Eventually the news is going to get out. This and this only has been my appointed work: getting this news to those who have never heard of God, and explaining how it works by simple faith and plain truth. Since prayer is at the bottom of all this, what I want mostly is for men to pray."

We should pray for our fellow believers, too. We're instructed to do just that by Jesus himself in Matthew 9:35–38: "Jesus went through all the towns and villages, teaching in their synagogues, preaching the good news of the kingdom and healing every disease and sickness. When he saw the crowds, he had compassion on them, because they were harassed and helpless, like sheep without a shepherd. Then he said to his disciples, 'The harvest is plentiful but the workers are few. Ask the Lord of the harvest, therefore, to send out workers into his harvest field.'"

Fellow harvesters come through prayer. Boldness to witness comes through prayer. Opportunities to share also come through prayer. Ask him to give you an opportunity to share his message of love and hope with someone this week. Then keep your eyes open for the answer. That happens to be a prayer the Lord delights in answering.

Paul even asked for prayer that the Lord would bring opportunities for him to share Jesus in prison in Colossians 4:3: "And pray for us, too, that God may open a door for our message, so that we may proclaim the mystery of Christ, for which I am in chains." In the next verse, Paul asked for prayer that he would be clear. "Pray that I may proclaim it clearly, as I should." Don't you just love the way God answered Paul's prayer in such an enormous way? A couple thousand years later, people are still affected by the doors the Lord opened for Paul to share. We're still affected by the way God used him to share it so clearly.

Ask Good Questions

Does the person with whom you're sharing understand that salvation happens only through Christ? Does she understand that she can't earn her way to heaven and into a right relationship with God? Many don't. You can get a dialogue going by saying something like this: "I'd love to hear your take on what it is that can bring us to a right relationship with God and what it takes to get to heaven." Ask questions about the person's beliefs. If she answers anything apart from faith in Jesus, then she needs to hear what real salvation is all about. While you're asking questions, ask if you could share your view of how a person can get to heaven. If she's not interested, that's the signal it's time to back off and do some more praying. Jesus wasn't pushy. He chose to hang around those who wanted to be with him, those who wanted to hear—even if they were tax collectors and prostitutes, the lowlifes of the day. Not only should we guard against being pushy, we should guard against being judgmental. I need to ask myself, now and then, if there's anyone I wouldn't be willing to share Christ with. Chocolate snobbery is one thing. But that kind of selectiveness should never ooze over into the way we share our faith. His love is for everyone.

If you're sharing with a person who isn't ready to listen, pray that the Lord will do a softening work in her heart by his Holy Spirit and that he will give her the willingness to hear and the faith to respond. Pray for an open door.

On the other hand, the Holy Spirit may already have started a work in her heart. She may have just been waiting for you to offer to share with her how she can find forgiveness and eternal life. If you ask if you can share, and the person expresses a willingness to listen, praise God for the open door and charge on through!

Be Gracious

In our sharing, we need to be careful not to condemn or belittle—even if the person we're witnessing to shares beliefs that are totally "out there." We need to be kind and loving. Colossians 4:5–6 (MSG) says, "Use your heads as you live and work among outsiders. Don't miss a trick. Make the most of every opportunity. Be gracious in your speech. The goal is to bring out the best in others in a conversation, not put them down, not cut them out."

Share Simply

Share in your clearest, everyday language about God's holiness. Tell the people you're sharing with how much God loves them and that he wants them for his own children.

Then share about the problem of sin, breaking God's laws. Since he's so holy and can't have fellowship with sin, and we've all sinned (see Rom. 3:23), that puts us in dire need of a Savior. In John 3:16, we're told plainly about the Savior who meets our needs: "For God so *loved* that he *gave!*" Ephesians 1:7 tells us that "In him we have redemption through his blood, the forgiveness of sins." What a privilege it is to be able to tell others that Jesus is the answer to our sin problem.

If the person is willing, you can lead her in a prayer like the suggested prayer in the last chapter of this book. Help her to understand that the new life is a change of direction, giving over the controls of her life. Let her know that her decision is one that affects her life here and now, but it gives her an eternity in heaven, too. And if it's true that life is like a box of chocolates, then eternal life is the whole Wonka factory! Give her a little insight into the glorious future that awaits her. If it's at all possible, stick with your new sibling in Christ and help her to get established and going in the right direction in her new walk with Jesus.

Chocolate-covered Blessings

We can let sharing our faith with others be a thrilling reminder of what we've been given in Christ.

Philemon 1:6 says, "I pray that you may be active in sharing your faith, so that you will have a full understanding of every good thing we have in Christ." And we truly do have every good thing in the Lord. Praise him, the creator of everything good—the creator of chocolate!

I keep asking that the God of our Lord Jesus Christ, the glorious Father, may give you the Spirit of wisdom and revelation, so that you may know him better. I pray also that the eyes of your heart may be enlightened in order that you may know the hope to which he has called you, the riches of his glorious inheritance in the saints, and his incomparably great power for us who believe. That power is like the working of his mighty strength, which he exerted in Christ when he raised him from the dead and seated him at his right hand in the heavenly realms, far above all rule and authority, power and dominion, and every title that can be given, not only in the present age but also in the one to come.

Ephesians 1:17–21

part eight

The Rest of the Story

Learning to Rest in Christ

chapter thirty-six
Flap-happy

I was at the mall when I noticed a mob scene at a department store cosmetic counter. "What's all the flap about?" someone asked. "Two for one on 'Wrinkles-B-Gone Miracle Cream!" came a muffled cry from behind a sea of purses.

They definitely had my attention. Not only would I be a great candidate for a drum or two of Wrinkles-B-Gone, but I think I find the "flap" topic all the more interesting now that I'm over forty. I know a thing or two about flapping. But I'd really rather not focus on my upper arms, thank you. Thighs are out, too. When I'm forced to think about the jiggle situation, I'm reminded of what happened when I hit forty: It hit me back.

Major Meltdown

I experienced a bit of a forties meltdown—and "meltdown" is a pretty accurate description. Have you ever seen a candle that's been burning a while? Everything sort of oozes down to the bottom. That's forty. I think it started at the face. A good percentage of my face is now sort of "pooling" around my chin. Not pretty. It's my own, sad "Candle in the Wind" ballad. And I didn't even need the wind.

I guess we might as well face it ("face" it?)—faces and bodies are almost always destined to experience a bit of a midlife landslide. We can fight it with industrial strength wrinkle creams, injections, surgeries, super glue, or whatever the age-defying cure du jour might be, but few of us will ever look twenty again. Trying to hang on to the twenty-look is like wrestling with the wind. And I should warn you to be careful when wrestling the wind. It can snuff out your candle altogether.

The Windblown Look

Even though the wind is a candle's enemy, there are scores of positive things it does for us. It cools us on a warm day, scatters seeds, sails boats, and can even generate some of the juice that operates our blow-dryers.

Have you ever seen a dog riding with his head hanging out of a car window? It always makes me feel just a little better about my own jiggly-face situation. Dogs seem to know how to get a kick out of wind resistance vs. jiggle face.

And how about birds? Not only do they enjoy the wind, they use it to allow them to soar. Most birds, anyway. Chickens seem to be more interested in flapping, fluttering, and making noise than they do in soaring. They never even get off the ground.

Soaring vs. Flapping

Our heavenly Father wants us to soar. We tend to think we need to flap and squawk and wrestle the wind. But I'd rather be an eagle than a chicken. If you've ever seen an eagle soar, you might've noticed that it's not really the flapping that keeps him in the air. It's his resting and trusting the wind, allowing the wind to push beneath his wings—that's what keeps the eagle in flight.

We don't need to fret and flap, either. When we're resting in Christ, all the little flaps of life don't seem nearly so big. And when we stop focusing on all the fretful things of life, we're able to get things done for the Lord. We really take off! Isaiah 40:31 says, "But those who hope in the LORD will renew their strength. They will soar on wings like eagles; they will run and not grow weary, they will walk and not be faint."

When the Soaring Gets Tough . . .

What did God remind the children of Israel in Exodus 19:3–4, after they had left Egypt? "Then Moses went up to God, and the LORD called to him from the mountain and said, 'This is what you are to say to the house of Jacob and what you are to tell the people of Israel: 'You yourselves have seen what I did to Egypt, and how I carried you on eagles' wings and brought you to myself.'"

The children of Israel hadn't exactly had the smoothest of rides out of Egypt. But God told them to remember how he carried them on eagles' wings and brought them to himself. Even when the ride gets rough, there is certain rest for those who will trust the Lord. And we can rejoice that our souls are eternally safe, completely covered in soft, titanium-type God-feathers.

Safely Soaring

There's no safer place to be than resting in our faithful Father. Psalm 91:1–2 (HCSB) says, "The one who lies under the protection of the Most High dwells in the shadow of the Almighty."'

Rest in the Lord. He is faithful to take care of you. Psalm 91 tells us that "He will cover you with His feathers; you will take refuge under His wings. His faithfulness will be a protective shield" (v. 4 HCSB).

There's nothing wrong with trying the cure du jour if you're brave enough. But trusting in Jesus we find ourselves safely tucked under his wings. Jesus said in Matthew 11:28–29 (HCSB), "Come to Me, all you who are weary and burdened, and I will give you rest. Take My yoke upon you and learn from Me, because I am gentle and humble in heart, and you will find rest for your souls."

We can soar under his power instead of our own wind-wrestling wimpiness. It's amazing that when we find rest and safety in him, we find a new strength— spiritual muscle galore! It's more thrilling than a two-fer at the cosmetic counter.

Jesus resumed talking to the people, but now tenderly. "The Father has given me all these things to do and say. This is a unique Father-Son operation, coming out of Father and Son intimacies and knowledge. No one knows the Son the way the Father does, nor the Father the way the Son does. But I'm not keeping it to myself; I'm ready to go over it line by line with anyone willing to listen.

"Are you tired? Worn out? Burned out on religion? Come to me. Get away with me and you'll recover your life. I'll show you how to take a real rest. Walk with me and work with me—watch how I do it. Learn the unforced rhythms of grace. I won't lay anything heavy or ill-fitting on you. Keep company with me and you'll learn to live freely and lightly."

Matthew 11:27–30, THE MESSAGE

chapter thirty-seven
I'll Fly Away

I had one of those purgatory-type flights recently. The flight was delayed for over an hour, so I missed my connecting flight. They put me on standby for the next one and after a marathon layover, I made it onto the last leg home by the skin of my teeth. Then after I finally boarded the plane and everything was finally set, the airline powers-that-be realized our plane had too much fuel. So we sat for another hour in the hot, stuffy plane while the gas guys sucked out the extra ton or two. I got home about five hours later than I had planned. The good news is that I did get home. Too many of these stories don't have the same kind of happy ending.

Clipped at Security

As a matter of fact, I know for sure it could've been worse. As we sat on the stationary plane, one guy told us about how he had gotten nabbed in security on one of his flights for a pair of contraband *nose hair clippers*. Let me quickly add that I completely understand the need for heightened security in our airports. I support it and cooperate. But I have to admit I had to snicker when I tried to picture those nose hair clippers as a threat to our national security.

Can you imagine a poor, clueless perpetrator? "I've got a pair of nose hair clippers—and I know how to use 'em!" Or how about, "Stand back or I'll trim your nose hair within an inch of your life!" I don't mean to be tacky, but it seems to me that any guy who would try to hijack a plane with nose hair clippers would be a couple of commuters shy of a full passenger manifest. Could he really be a threat to anyone's security? Wouldn't this be the kind of guy who would actually *listen* when the flight attendants give instructions in the fine art of seatbelt buckling? "Insert what? Where?" I have to tell you, I would have a hard time being afraid of this kind of guy.

Truly Secure Flight

I was thinking on that near-eternal flight that it's nice to know there really is nothing to fear when I fly. I know that Jesus is with me. Okay, I may have gotten just a little uneasy when I remembered that the Lord said, *"Low* I am with you always."

Don't worry, that's a little joke. I really do know exactly where Jesus is. He's right here in my heart. And as complicated as it may sound, at the same time he's in my heart, I'm tucked safely in his hand. Ephesians 3:16–17 says, "I pray that out of his glorious riches he may strengthen you with power through his Spirit in your inner being, so that Christ may dwell in your hearts through faith." Christ is dwelling right here in my heart. And Jesus himself said in John 10:27–29, "My sheep listen to my voice; I know them, and they follow me. I give them eternal life, and they shall never perish; no one can snatch them out of my hand. My Father, who has given them to me, is greater than all; no one can snatch them out of my Father's hand."

How could I feel any safer than the security I enjoy when I understand that he's in me and all around me, and I'm nestled in his all-powerful and ever-loving hand? Now *this* is heightened security—hijacker-proof!

The next verse in the Ephesians 3 passage continues with Paul's prayer for us: "And I pray that you, being rooted and established in love, may have power, together with all the saints, to grasp how wide and long and high and deep is the love of Christ" (v. 18). Excuse me, did that say *high?* How wonderful to know that I'm safe in all directions, from the friendly skies down!

Both Feet Firmly Planted ... in the Air?

We don't need our feet firmly planted on the ground to have security in this instance. We need to have our feet—well, really our *hearts*—firmly planted in the love of Christ. "And I ask him that with both feet planted firmly on love, you'll be able to take in with all Christians the extravagant dimensions of Christ's love. Reach out and experience the breadth! Test its length! Plumb the depths! Rise to the heights!" (Eph. 3:17–18 MSG).

I'm so delighted that these are heights I can rise to without a plane. I also feel so much safer about flying now that I know I'm safe from any and all rogue nose hair clippers. The guy who got stuck in security ended up donating his clippers to the cause. We call him "Fur Nose" now.

As you read over what I have written to you, you'll be able to see for yourselves into the mystery of Christ. None of our ancestors understood this. Only in our time has it been made clear by God's Spirit through his holy apostles and prophets of this new order. The mystery is that people who have never heard of God and those who have heard of him all their lives (what I've been calling outsiders and insiders) stand on the same ground before God. They get the same offer, same help, same promises in Christ Jesus. The Message is accessible and welcoming to everyone, across the board. ...

My response is to get down on my knees before the Father, this magnificent Father who parcels out all heaven and earth. I ask him to strengthen you by his Spirit—not a brute strength but a glorious inner strength—that Christ will live in you as you open the door and invite him in. And I ask him that with both feet planted firmly on love, you'll be able to take in with all Christians the extravagant dimensions of Christ's love. Reach out and experience the breadth! Test its length! Plumb the depths! Rise to the heights!

Ephesians 3:4–6, 14–18, THE MESSAGE

chapter thirty-eight
. . . . .
Not by Sight

I was out shopping recently and I decided to try on a pair of jeans. For the record, a jeans fitting should never be done on the spur of the moment. One should carefully calculate and prepare for such a thing—maybe even get a little counseling beforehand. I made one of those surprise jeans stops. It was right after lunch. What in the world was I thinking?

Too Much to Stomach

I'd call the jeans about a 98-percent fit. I should've been thankful. After all, if that were a grade, it would be a high A. But those dreaded leftovers—just two percent or so—were causing a major problem. Just a few leftover ounces caused a sort of ooze out the top of the jeans. When I checked it out in the mirror, the whole gruesome picture gave me a sort of Jabba the Hutt visual. I worked to force the Jabba two-percent down into the jeans, but the force was definitely not with me. It was not one of my better dressing-room moments. It's bad enough when I have to struggle to tuck in a shirt, but I especially hate it when I have to struggle to tuck in my stomach. Not just "suck it in," but really and truly "tuck it in." What a sight!

What a Faith!

Thankfully, I'm informed in 2 Corinthians 5:7 that "We live by faith, not by sight." In the dressing room, I can get the tiniest inkling of how much better faith is than sight. Hebrews 11:6 says, "And without faith it is impossible to please God, because anyone who comes to him must believe that he exists and that he rewards those who earnestly seek him." Living by faith means I'm pleasing God. And who would I rather please anyway, the mirror or the Creator of the universe?

Fixing Our Eyes

Hebrews 11 teaches us what faith is. In verse one, it says, "Now faith is being sure of what we hope for and certain of what we do not see." I love the way *The Message* describes this faith: "The fundamental fact of existence is that this trust in God, this faith, is the firm foundation under everything that makes life worth living. It's our handle on what we can't see. The act of faith is what distinguished our ancestors, set them above the crowd. By faith, we see the world called into existence by God's word, what we see created by what we don't see" (Heb. 11:1–3).

The next chapter tells us just how to get it and where it comes from: "Let us fix our eyes on Jesus, the author and perfecter of our faith" (Heb. 12:2). Faith comes as our eyes are fixed on Jesus, and not on the temporary (and often disturbing) things we can see in this world. He's the author, the originator of our faith, and he's the one who will perfect it.

What I can see with my eyes is temporary (a Jabba-sized sigh of relief). The things in life that really matter are eternal—and I can't see them in any dressing room mirror. They're matters of the heart. Jesus has mine. What a weight that lifts! Okay, maybe it doesn't lift the two-percent overflow weight, but our eternal glory far "outweighs" any earthly nuisance we can imagine: "Therefore we do not lose heart. Though outwardly we are wasting away, yet inwardly we are being renewed day by day. For our light and momentary troubles are achieving for us an eternal glory that far outweighs them all. So we fix our eyes not on what is seen, but on what is unseen. For what is seen is temporary, but what is unseen is eternal" (2 Cor. 4:16–18).

Come in for a Focus Treatment

When the "outward wasting away" part of the passage catches our focus, that's when we know it's time for a good inward renewing. About how often do we need it? "Day by day." The renewing isn't a spa treatment. It's not a wrap. Not even a fancy diet. As a matter of fact, we don't do it at all. Jesus Christ himself takes care of the renewing for us. When he renews us, he makes us look like him—perfectly beautiful. By faith, we can know that the Lord has trimmed away every creepy part of our inner life and made us brand, spanking new on the inside, where it really counts.

Fix the Focus

Focus on the two-percent overflow? Nope. As a matter of fact, I should never focus on the 98 percent either. My focus should be on the innards, not the "outwards"—and that focus needs to remain fixed. In both Hebrews 12:2 and again in 2 Corinthians 4:18 we're instructed to "fix our eyes" on Jesus, on the unseen. That's the way to live by faith, not by sight.

That's how I want to live. Living by faith and not by sight will make life better in every way—especially if I happen to come across another *Star Wars* sighting in the dressing room.

We're not keeping this quiet, not on your life. Just like the psalmist who wrote, "I believed it, so I said it," we say what we believe. And what we believe is that the One who raised up the Master Jesus will just as certainly raise us up with you, alive. Every detail works to your advantage and to God's glory: more and more grace, more and more people, more and more praise!

So we're not giving up. How could we! Even though on the outside it often looks like things are falling apart on us, on the inside, where God is making new life, not a day goes by without his unfolding grace. These hard times are small potatoes compared to the coming good times, the lavish celebration prepared for us. There's far more here than meets the eye. The things we see now are here today, gone tomorrow. But the things we can't see now will last forever.

2 Corinthians 4:13–18, THE MESSAGE

chapter thirty-nine
. . . . .
Christian Soup for the Chicken Soul

Why do my teenagers get a kick out of those fear-inducing shows? I tried to watch part of that *Fear Factor* show one time. I had to stop when my left eye started to twitch. If I had to choose either being subjected to one of their gross-out/torture situations or being subjected to watching the show, I'm not sure which I'd choose. A program with the sole purpose of terrifying the socks off its participants while thoroughly disgusting its audience is just not my cup of soup.

The Gross Quotient

Besides, I'm a mom. It would take a completely different kind of "fear factor" for parents, don't you think? We've been desensitized to most gross-out situations.

I remember waking to the "I think I'm gonna ... !" call in the middle of one night. My husband sprinted to the boys' room. Adrenaline pumping, he stretched his arms ceiling-ward and hoisted a pale six-year-old out of the top bunk. But just as he had him directly overhead (picture a target painted on top of his head), it was all over. All over my husband (poor Richie). All over the carpet, too (poor me). Until those program execs have experienced a middle-of-the-night barf shower and the toxic cleanup thereafter, they really don't have much of a handle on the parent factor.

The Mom Factor

What kind of show would they have to put together for mothers in particular? For one thing, I think we moms could top anything they could come up with in two syllables: childbirth. In addition, moms have already had experiences that top out the gross-out/danger scale. Picture a mom fishing a cricket from her toddler's mouth (or worse, *half* a cricket). Imagine her wading through a minefield of Legos and jacks. Envision her easing her teen's closet door open only to be buried alive in an eruption of decomposing laundry—including sweat socks that have been smoldering in a sort of laundry compost for a couple of weeks. Sorry, program exec guys. You can't scare this woman.

On the other hand, if they considered a show staged around a husband inviting spur-of-the-moment guests over after church on Sunday, they might get closer to a fear-inducing mom moment. They could get the adrenaline pumping if they had one of the guests open their teen's closet door. If that guest happened to be Martha Stewart, they might really have something. Or how about a "step on the scales after the holidays" challenge? Now we're talking about a measurable fear factor.

Christian Soup Mix

Thankfully, being a believer puts us in a whole different mix. Instead of "stewing" about the troublesome circumstances life dishes out, we have another choice. We can trade fear for peace when we trade fret and worry for prayer. In Philippians 4:6–7 (MSG), we find these instructions: "Don't fret or worry. Instead of worrying, pray. Let petitions and praises shape your worries into prayers, letting God know your concerns. Before you know it, a sense of God's wholeness, everything coming together for good, will come and settle you down. It's wonderful what happens when Christ displaces worry at the center of your life."

We've heard of being pear-shaped. (That's a completely different fear-inducing topic.) But what we really want to aim for is being "prayer-shaped." "Let petitions and praises shape your worries into prayers" (v. 4). As our lives are shaped by prayer and praise instead of fret and fear, God comes and "settles us down" with his perfect peace.

The Real Courage Factor

Picture the great apostle Peter wimping out. One minute he was telling Jesus he would die for him, the next minute he was too afraid to stand up for his Lord even to a little servant girl. Fast forward to the Peter who shook up the world with his bold preaching. He's the Peter who faced beatings and the threat of death with every word, but shared Christ and stood fearlessly for him anyway all the rest of his life. What happened?

The Comforter happened. Peter was changed when the Holy Spirit came to indwell him. From wimpy zero to fearless hero—it was as if he consumed a giant helping of courage soup.

Ladle on the Courage with the Right Kind of Fear

The Bible does remind us of a good kind of fear. It's a fear that leads to life, according to Proverbs 19:23—the fear of God. Fearing God includes honoring and respecting him, being in complete awe of him. Proverbs 10:27 says, "The fear of the Lord adds length to life." and Psalm 111:10 tells us that "The fear of the Lord is the beginning of wisdom." The right kind of fear can lead us to a solid trust in the Lord. The more we trust, the more we know we can have No Fear!

As we walk in the Spirit and enjoy his indwelling presence, we can live without the bad fear just as Peter did. Psalm 56:3 says, "When I am afraid, I will trust in you."

We don't have to worry what will happen to us when we're trusting the Lord. We can rest in his Spirit and live without feeling trapped in the fears of our circumstances. Psalm 23:4 says, "Even though I walk through the valley of the shadow of death, I will fear no evil, for you are with me; your rod and your staff, they comfort me." I can live without fear because the Comforter is with me. Our Father told us himself in Isaiah 41:10, "So do not fear, for I am with you."

Would you believe, we don't even have to be nervous? Psalm 112:6–8 gives us the "no fear" charge: "Surely he will never be shaken; a righteous man will be remembered forever. He will have no fear of bad news; his heart is steadfast, trusting in the LORD. His heart is secure, he will have no fear; in the end he will look in triumph on his foes."

So there's no need for you to be shaken. Keep your heart steadfast, trusting in the Lord.

Be unafraid. Be very unafraid.

Light, space, zest—that's GOD! So, with him on my side I'm fearless, afraid of no one and nothing. When vandal hordes ride down ready to eat me alive, Those bullies and toughs fall flat on their faces. When besieged, I'm calm as a baby. When all hell breaks loose, I'm collected and cool.

Psalm 27:1–3, THE MESSAGE

chapter forty
Nine Lives

I've heard it said that the difference between dogs and cats is that dogs have owners, cats have *staff*. We recently sort of misplaced our cat. We (the staff) looked everywhere for him. We like to call it a "cat scan." We finally located him—guess where. On top of the refrigerator!

I have to confess, I might not have been searching for the cat as diligently as my children were. It's not that I don't love good, ol' Sammy. But I can't deny he makes a lot of work for me. Even if you ignore the box, the vet, and the unspeakable hairball events, there's still the matter of the fur. Every time he hauls his chunky body off the floor (where he's usually parked for hours at a time), he leaves behind a hair clump the size of a gerbil. The other day, out of the corner of my eye, I thought I saw an entire gerbil herd grazing on my living room carpet. I'm praying they don't stampede.

Kids + Cat = Trouble

Add kids to the cat picture and you're talking about even more work. When you have kids and cats in the same house, you have to watch both carefully. Children seem to love to cover cats with shortening, toothpaste, and/or Vapo-rub. Kids also usually feel the need to give the cat a bubble bath, and they somehow think every cat would enjoy a good fluff from a ride in the dryer.

After you convince the kids that cats really don't appreciate bubbles or drying (even on the gentle cycle), they often take that to mean they should clean the cat with the Dustbuster. I'm not sure that the cat's method of cleaning himself wasn't more of a defense mechanism than an instinct.

Bad Cat-itude

It's not only that Sammy makes extra work for me, either. No, there's an attitude at work that really gets on my nerves. He gives me "the look." I've also seen it on several teenagers (never any of mine, of course). It's a sort of condescending look of superiority. Whatever I ask him to do—and what a waste of time that is—he looks at me as if to indicate that whatever I'm asking is entirely beneath him. Someone reminded me that thousands of years ago people worshiped cats. I don't think Sammy has ever quite gotten past that.

Overwhelming Love

What is it that makes the kids love the cat? Pretty much nothing. They require nothing, yet love Sammy overwhelmingly.

God loves us overwhelmingly and unconditionally, too. It's that unconditional love of his that makes him want you for his own. Isn't it awesome to be loved and wanted? He loves and wants you so much that even though you were separated from him by sin, he made a plan to win you back.

Every one of us needs to be "won back"—all of us have sinned. Romans 3:10–11 says, "There is no one righteous, not even one; there is no one who understands, no one who seeks God." We've, in essence, given God "the look." But even though we were arrogant and unlovable, Jesus came as part of God's unconditional love plan. "But God demonstrates his own love for us in this: While we were still sinners, Christ died for us" (Rom. 5:8). We were lost—to the top of the fridge times eternity—when God came looking for us through his Son. Jesus lived a sinless life and died a sacrificial death on the cross to pay our sin penalty. Romans 3:23–25 says, "For all have sinned and fall short of the glory of God, and are justified freely by his grace through the redemption that came by Christ Jesus. God presented him as a sacrifice of atonement, through faith in his blood."

Got Righteousness?

When he died on the cross, he was taking the punishment for every sin you've ever committed—past, present, and future. Once you've accepted Christ, you're declared righteous in the eyes of God. Romans 3:22 says, "This righteousness from God comes through faith in Jesus Christ to all who believe." Three days after Jesus died, he rose from the dead, conquering sin and death once and for all. He's alive! And when we ask him to forgive our sin and to come into our lives and take control, he does just that. We can believe the promise of Romans 10:13: "Everyone who calls on the name of the Lord will be saved."

When we give him our lives, he makes us new. Isn't it wonderful that God loves us without strings (or even yarn balls)? His unconditional, selfless, sacrificing, extravagant love has made new life possible for all who will receive him—eternal life. That's nine lives *times forever!*

A Special Note to My Friends Who've Not Yet Given Their Lives to Christ

If you've never responded to God's unconditional love, you can do it this very moment. It doesn't matter where you are or what you're doin. If you've never given your life to Christ, this could be the moment that changes your eternal destiny. If you haven't yet surrendered your life to him, I'm convinced it's no accident that God has brought you to this place—or to this *page*.

Would you like to get in on the forever life? Let Jesus know about it. You can pray something like this:

"Father, I know I've sinned. I believe you sent your Son to die on the cross to pay for everything I've ever done wrong. I trust you right now to give me a clean slate—to forgive every sin. Thank you for forgiving me and for loving me so overwhelmingly—even as much as you love your Son, Jesus. Thank you for treasuring me as someone worthwhile—even as someone precious. I give you my life and my all. I pray you'll help me to become more and more like Jesus and that you'll use me in whatever way you want to bring glory to yourself for the rest of my life. Thank you for saving me. In Jesus' name, Amen."

If you just prayed this kind of prayer for the first time, your life has been radically and eternally changed. Sin? Outta here! New life? Yours! Let someone know what's going on in your life. Let a solid believer help you as you get started in your new walk with Christ. And let me be the first to welcome you as a real Ya-Ya sister of the heart!

How blessed is God! And what a blessing he is! He's the Father of our Master, Jesus Christ, and takes us to the high places of blessing in him. Long before he laid down earth's foundations, he had us in mind, had settled on us as the focus of his love, to be made whole and holy by his love. Long, long ago he decided to adopt us into his family through Jesus Christ. (What pleasure he took in planning this!) He wanted us to enter into the celebration of his lavish gift-giving by the hand of his beloved Son.

Because of the sacrifice of the Messiah, his blood poured out on the altar of the Cross, we're a free people—free of penalties and punishments chalked up by all our misdeeds. And not just barely free, either. Abundantly *free! He thought of everything, provided for everything we could possibly need, letting us in on the plans he took such delight in making. He set it all out before us in Christ, a long-range plan in which everything would be brought together and summed up in him, everything in deepest heaven, everything on planet earth.*

It's in Christ that we find out who we are and what we are living for.

Ephesians 1:3–11, THE MESSAGE

notes

• • • • •

Chapter 22:

1. Rick Warren, *The Purpose Driven® Life—What on Earth Am I Here For?* (Grand Rapids, Mich.: Zondervan, 2000), 31.

Chapter 28:

1. Carolyn Arends, "Seize the Day" on *I Can Hear You,* © 1995, Sunday Shoes Music (ASCAP).Used by permission.

Readers' Guide

For Personal Reflection
or Group Discussion

Part One: The Prayer Necessities

Chapter One: Pump It Up

1. Rhonda glanced at a photo and saw a chubby woman wearing a suit just like hers. Realizing the plump woman was none other than herself, she vowed to get into shape. When Christians get out of spiritual fitness there are consequences just as noticeable as being twenty pounds overweight. What are the areas in your life that fall apart when you don't pray or do "soul aerobics"?

2. This chapter outlines Rhonda's attempt to get in shape physically and describes that she felt like she had fallen into a paper shredder after taking an aerobics class. Discipline in any area requires some sort of sacrifice. What are the sacrifices you need to make in order to remain vigorous and vital in your prayer life?

3. There are many parallels between becoming physically fit and developing the spiritual discipline of prayer. In what ways is prayer superior to physical training? (See 1 Timothy 4:7–10 for some hints.)

4. Applying the principles of "soul aerobics" results in giving God control of your life. First Timothy 4:8 describes godliness as "profitable" for all things. Describe some of the good things that happen when you build a spiritual connection with God by praying moment by moment.

Chapter Two: Can We Talk?

1. In this chapter Rhonda notes that her children are more likely to initiate a conversation when they need something. What is your main motivation for initiating a conversation—praying—to your heavenly Father? Are your prayers need-based?

2. Rhonda calls asking God for things the "grocery list kind of prayer." Praying in this way is fine; Scripture supports it in James 4:2: "You do not have, because you do not ask God." Even Jesus instructed us to pray, "Give us today our daily bread" (Matt. 6:11). Asking for things, however, should be only a small part of your prayers to God. According to Rhonda, what should be the main motivation for prayer?

3. Romans 12:11–12 says, "Never be lacking in zeal, but keep your spiritual fervor, serving the Lord. Be joyful in hope, patient in affliction, faithful in prayer." When you are busy, should you be spending more time or less time in prayer?

4. According to Rhonda, when you pour your energies into keeping your connection to the Lord flourishing, what are the results?

5. The chapter ends with a passage from the book of James, which tells us we should pray when we are sick and when we need spiritual healing. "The prayer of a righteous man is powerful and effective" (5:16). In which areas of your life do you need "powerful and effective" prayer?

Chapter Three: The Power of PMS

1. This chapter tells about the power of "Prayer and Meditation in Solitude"—or PMS. Even though it is the most powerful force imaginable on earth, PMS does not guarantee a change in your circumstances or situation. What is PMS guaranteed to change?

2. If you want extraordinary things to happen in your life, what does Rhonda recommend in the section titled "Power Hour"? Who is responsible for making you willing to follow God's purpose?

3. Believers are to pray "continually," says 1 Thessalonians 5:17. What should be your attitude of prayer, according to Jeremiah 29:12–13?

4. Beginning a time of prayer is like dialing God's phone number. The psalms suggest certain ways to begin that conversation. What are they?

5. Effective prayer also includes a time of confession and thanksgiving. Giving thanks in all circumstances is God's will for us (1 Thess. 5:18). We are encouraged to pray in sincere thankfulness for difficult situations. What are those tough areas in your life? How should you be tackling them through prayer?

6. It really is okay to ask God for things when you pray. But mature Christians shouldn't keep their lists focused on themselves. What and whom should you be praying for? What will be the results of that type of prayer?

7. Rhonda points out that there is so much power in prayer and "so little time" to use it. She says, "When we persist in getting alone with the Lord and spending time with him in prayer, we can see great things happen. It's the kind of PMS we all need." What are some of the great things you'd like to see happen through PMS?

Chapter Four: Have I Reached the Party to Whom I Am Speaking?

1. In this chapter, Rhonda likens prayer to having God's cell phone number. We can call him anytime, anyplace. No voice mail. No busy signal. We always have an instant connection. God's line is always open. There are some things, however, that can give us technical difficulties. What are the two things Rhonda mentions that may cause "static interference"?

2. According to Psalm 66:18, sin is a big cause of prayer interference: "If I had cherished sin in my heart, the Lord would not have listened." It's not that God doesn't care about us. He is not powerless or deaf; he still loves us. Why, then, does unconfessed sin disconnect us from God?

3. If we want God to "closely attend" to our prayers as described in Proverbs 15:29, what do we need to do?

4. The second cause of prayer "static" Rhonda notes is unforgiveness. What is the "prayer/forgiveness connection" as outlined in Matthew 6:14–15 and Mark 11:25?

Chapter Five: Urgent Assistance Needed

1. The opening of the chapter describes emails Rhonda has received from wealthy diplomats and dignitaries who are looking to give away money. Even though these emails are a scam, they appeal to a universal, basic human desire—the desire for treasure. Rhonda notes that even God desires treasure. What are the things that God treasures according to Psalm 141:1–2 and Revelation 5:8?

2. God hangs onto our prayers like "a mom hangs her child's most special works on her refrigerator." Our words offered in prayer are more precious to the Father than we can imagine. How should this concept affect the way we pray?

3. In Matthew 6:19–20 Jesus told us to invest in eternal, spiritual treasures. According to Rhonda, what is one way we can store up our heavenly treasures?

4. Every person is just one of a gajillion people seeking God's attention. According to Rhonda, why does God listen to each of us in a special way?

5. In 1 Timothy 2:1–10 (MSG), the apostle Paul exhorted us to pray and finished with "I want women to get in there with the men in humility before God, not primping before a mirror or chasing the latest fashions but doing something beautiful for God and becoming beautiful doing it." Other things besides worrying about looks can capture our hearts. What are the things in your life that distract you from prayer?

Part Two: Hope for the Directionally Impaired

Chapter Six: On the Road Again

1. Rhonda describes herself as "directionally impaired." She has an uncanny talent for getting lost, even in a parking lot. Sometimes we all can develop an uncanny talent for getting spiritually lost. What is the only road map for finding our spiritual bearings?

2. "It's tough to stay headed in the direction of the kingdom when we're fixed on an earthly compass," says Rhonda in the section "Need Directions?" If you want a joy-filled life packed with purpose, what does she recommend?

3. Finding God's purpose for your life isn't always easy. Sometimes we take detours and wind up on the road to nowhere. We're filled with that lost feeling and end up frustrated. Psalm 119:29–30 (MSG) reads, "Barricade the road that goes Nowhere; grace me with your clear revelation. I choose the true road to Somewhere; I post your road signs at every curve and corner. I grasp and cling to whatever you tell me; GOD, don't let me down! I'll run the course you lay out for me if you'll just show me how." Where are you headed right now in your spiritual life? Are you sitting at an intersection, looking at

your map?Are you on the road to Somewhere or to Nowhere?

4. What is the final destination for those going Somewhere?

Chapter Seven: Ya Better Believe It

1. Why can't we trust the TV when it tells us products like the Kitchen Magic Missile are a good deal?

2. Why is the Bible such a good deal? What can it do for our souls, according to Hebrews 4:12?

3. The Bible has been and will be trustworthy for thousands of generations. In the section "The Word on the Word," what proof does Rhonda cite for its authenticity?

4. If we read and meditate on the Bible, what will be the results?

5. Read Psalm 119:9–16 and jot down three creative ways you can do better to live according to God's Word.

Chapter Eight: The Plate-spinning Life

1. In this chapter, Rhonda uses a washing machine with an uneven load as an example of an unbalanced life. Balance is "the buzz" these days. When Rhonda's washer went whacko, she knew it because of the noise and the shaking. When your spiritual life is unbalanced, what are the tell-tale signs?

2. In the section "Spiritual Balance," Rhonda suggests a way for us to "readjust the load" so that our spiritual lives are better balanced. What does she say we need to do?

3. In order for our lives to be balanced in God's eyes, Rhonda says something "has to go." What is that?

4. All those hateful and evil acts throw our lives off-kilter. When we let go of sin, what are we to put into our lives? (Hint: see Galatians 5:16–25.)

5. This chapter quotes 2 Timothy 3:17 to show us how useful Scripture can be in our lives: "All Scripture is God-breathed and is useful for teaching, rebuking, correcting and training in righteousness, so that the man of God may be thoroughly equipped for every good work." By pursuing "training in righteousness" we can remain balanced. What are the areas in your life that need to be "trained" so that you can be balanced?

6. When Rhonda got her washing machine balanced, the adrenaline rush gave her energy to clean her house with some to spare. She facetiously said, "The neighbors got a little worried when I started doing their laundry, too." Imagine your life was perfectly balanced and you had spiritual energy to spare, what would you do with it?

Chapter Nine: Cover Story

1. "Cover Story" gives examples of two types of people: "coverers" and "users." Which type best represents your habits? Describe something you "cover"; describe something you "use."

2. Rhonda tells us that God's Word is to be "used." She wrote, "No need to save the treasure of his Word for a rainy day when we can use it every day." Do you consciously use the Bible every day? Do Scripture passages often run through your mind? Are you a Scripture "user"?

3. There's a point at which the Word of God "uncovers" our sins. Rhonda quotes Colossians 3:9–10: "Do not lie to each other, since you have taken off your old self with its practices and have put on the new self, which is being renewed in knowledge in the image of its Creator." What are we to take off? Is there a part of your old life that still needs to be "uncovered"?

4. "But the Lord didn't merely tell us what to take off and then leave us coverless," Rhonda assures us. "... He told us what to put on." The list in Colossians 3:12–15 tells us to put on "compassion, kindness, humility, gentleness and patience ... And over all these virtues put on love, which binds them all together in perfect unity." How do we take off the old, undesirable life? How do we put on compassion, love, and the like?

Chapter Ten: Some-bunny Stop Me!

1. Rhonda is convinced the bunny in her yard studies the art of garden raiding. Our instruction book is the Bible, and it gives us everything we need for living life the way it is meant to be lived. She gives us four questions to ensure we're getting the most out of our instruction manual. The first is "Am I spending the right amount of time in God's Word?" If you're not, what are you missing out on according to Rhonda?

2. When we study the Bible, Rhonda warns us about reading things into the passage that aren't there. Ask yourself the second question: "What is the passage I've read really saying?" She doesn't want us to neglect the obvious meaning the Bible author had in mind. What does she recommend studying in order to get the right meaning out of Scripture?

3. The third question to ask yourself while studying Scripture is "What is God saying to me through this passage?" She asks us to look for four different things. What are they?

4. After reading the Bible, we should ask ourselves, "Is there a verse or passage I should meditate on or memorize?" What are the benefits of Bible memorization according to Rhonda? According to Psalm 119:11?

Part Three: The Ya-Ya Ties That Bind

Chapter Eleven: Ups and Downs

1. In this chapter, Rhonda tells us she's afraid of getting on a trampoline. But she's not afraid to face the "ups and downs" of life. Why not? What benefit is there in having troubles or being in a "down" phase?

2. In the section "The Up-side," Rhonda quotes 2 Corinthians 1:3–5 to assure us that the Lord's comfort reaches beyond any hurt we may have. Are there areas of hurt in your life that you haven't trusted God to heal? Do you have hope that the Lord is close to the brokenhearted (as expressed in Psalm 34:17–20)?

3. "Knowing that the Father of Compassion is ready with comfort in mass quantity can add a little bounce to any day," Rhonda reminds us. Additionally, 2 Corinthians 4:15–18 tells us that our earthly struggles are light and momentary—temporary. What problems do you have that do not seem to be temporary? How are your troubles of today building eternal glory for you?

4. When we receive a full measure of God's comfort, what are we supposed to do with it? (Hint: See 2 Corinthians 1:3–5 MSG at the end of the chapter.)

Chapter Twelve: Diet Church

1. In the section entitled "'Full-service' Service" Rhonda describes a drive-through church where "you could choose a topic from the menu, order, then pay your tithe at the window, pick up your 'sermon-in-a-minute' tapes and be on your way. I can see the ad now: 'Church in thirty minutes or less, or it's free!'" What values in our society make a church like this seem attractive? Have you ever been disgruntled because your church's worship service didn't exactly meet your needs? What changes did you feel were necessary? How did you help in those changes?

2. If church were easy, would it work better? Rhonda points out that "Jesus didn't call us to an easy way. He called us to a 'most excellent way,' in 1 Corinthians 12:31." What is at the core of this "most excellent" church?

3. Whether or not we like it, the Lord's plan for his church includes loving each other, sharing with each other, and bearing with one another. Rhonda says, "Real church involves people. It involves loving them. It involves work—even sacrifice." According to Ephesians 4:16—"From him [Christ] the whole body, joined and held together by every supporting ligament, grows and builds itself up in love, as each part does its work"—what is the key to having a healthy church?

4. Rhonda points out that every earthly church is full of sinners—sinners who might need you to "spur" them on to love and good deeds. Being in a church and encouraging others is tough, but worth it. Are you part of a working body of believers? What are your goals for loving those in your church?

5. "Diet" churches don't work; they leave you empty and hollow like an empty Ding Dong. Christians are called to be full, but full of what per the section "The Ultimate Filling"?

Chapter Thirteen: The Last Laugh

1. Would Rhonda's Wal-Mart predicament have been easier to bear if she hadn't poked so much fun at her husband for the Taco Bell disaster? It probably seems harmless and humorous at the time, but when we laugh or judge others, ultimately we are lifting ourselves up. Why is this potentially harmful?

2. There's a boomerang philosophy described in this chapter relating to judging others. Rhonda says, "If you judge others, you'll find that judgment coming right back around and smacking you in the head." Whom are you tempted to pick on, criticize, or condemn? What may happen if you follow through on your impulses? Is avoiding humiliation the only reason we should be kind and lenient toward others?

3. John 8:16 is quoted in the section "Here Comes the Judge." Who is worthy to judge according to this passage?

4. Rhonda tells us that sometimes we are called—even commanded—to action if we see someone sinning. She says, "If, however, you lovingly and biblically confront someone who's involved in something that's clearly spelled out in Scripture as sin, that person may certainly feel judged." What is the difference between judging someone and confronting another Christian who is disobeying God's Word? What standard do we use when we confront someone about sin?

5. What action does Rhonda recommend if we want to stay away from a judgmental spirit?

Chapter Fourteen: Risk Ski Business

1. When Rhonda failed dismally on the bunny slopes, what made the humiliation easier to bear?

2. What does Rhonda recommend doing if you need a friend? How is that concept reinforced in the verse 1 Peter 4:8, which Rhonda quotes in the section "See What Develops."

3. "Loving a friend is not a one-time thing," Rhonda reminds us. "We're instructed to persevere in friendships." Describe someone who has been a persevering friend in your life, someone who has been there during your darkest hour. What can you learn from her/him?

4. There are certain people with whom we should not form close alliances. Who are they? (Hint: see 2 Corinthians 6:14.) Who are your closest friends? Do they lead you in the direction of the "light"? What criteria do you use when making new friends?

5. This chapter closes with Philippians 2:1–16. Read the passage and make a list of qualities you'd like in a friend. Read it again and make a list of qualities you need to develop in yourself.

Chapter Fifteen: Showers of Mercy

1. When Rhonda took a walk-through of her newly built home, she wanted to impress the builders with her knowledge. So, she inspected everything carefully—even the sink. While fiddling with the sprayer, she managed to douse her face and head with water. What lesson did she learn from this embarrassing situation?

2. Rhonda points out that God sends people into our lives to help us. A considerable portion of the Bible is dedicated to teaching us how to live with each other. For example, the Ten Commandments include helps for our relationship with God: don't have any other gods or make graven images, don't take his name in vain, set apart a holy day. Others deal with our relationships with family and friends: honor your parents, don't steal, don't murder

(even with a look that could kill), don't covet, don't commit adultery, don't lie. According to Rhonda, the fact that God spends so much time instructing us on relationships reveals two things—what are those two principles?

3. At the end of "Snap Out of It!" Rhonda wants you answer this question: If you did a spiritual walk-through of your life, searching out any relationship problems, what would you find? Do you have any hidden surprises waiting to spew in your face?

4. It really isn't enough just to avoid getting in squabbles. We're to be looking outward and seeking ways to help each other. Rhonda quotes 1 Thessalonians 5:11 to support this point. It says, "Therefore encourage one another and build each other up, just as in fact you are doing." Where are we to look for strength in order to fulfill this command?

5. Once we get the hang of building good relationships, Rhonda encourages us to seek excellence. She says, "We should all be maturing, becoming the examples and teachers ourselves." Are you an example of a loving, encouraging person? If not, in what relationship areas do you need to become more mature?

Part Four: The Spiritual Bifocals

Chapter Sixteen: In-Your-Face Grace

1. Rhonda is learning to live with a makeup kit the size of a toolbox. She's aging and coming to terms with her fleeting beauty. Examine where you are in your aging journey. Can you relate to her "trauma" when she sees herself upside down?

2. Read the passage at the end of the chapter, a portion of Proverbs 31, and consider this well-respected woman. Rhonda points out that her physical beauty is not mentioned in the passage. In your opinion, what is the most striking thing about her?

3. Rhonda notes that the Proverbs 31 woman "can laugh at the days to come." Does it seem to you that she is afraid of becoming old? Proverbs 31 says the woman does fear something; what is that?

4. "The true beauty of the Proverbs 31 woman is in her heart," says Rhonda. Do you spend more time in prayer or more time putting on your makeup? What are you doing in your life to ensure that your inner beauty surpasses your outer beauty?

5. In the section "This Semi-old House" Rhonda notes our bodies are the temple of the Holy Spirit and made for worship of our awesome Creator. "When we focus on him instead of our bodies," she says, "we can smile at the future, too, and we can put beauty in its proper perspective." Are you able to smile at the future, or do you need to allow God to help you put beauty in its proper perspective?

Chapter Seventeen: Such a Spectacle!

1. Rhonda's vision is so messed up she now has contacts so she can see far away, glasses so she can read when someone shoves papers under her nose, and another pair of glasses so she can see to find her contacts and/or her glasses. She can't even see an eye chart! But Rhonda is more concerned about her spiritual visual acuity. Clear focus to her means "the difference between keeping our lives on the right track and totally missing the chart." What does she say causes blurred spiritual vision?

2. Read Colossians 3:1–2 (MSG). According to that passage, what are we to focus on?

3. "There's a spiritual eye ailment we might call 'pressed-by-self-opia,'" Rhonda says. "It's a result of thinking we have to make things happen on our own, in our own strength." Do you have this "vision" problem? What things in your life do you need to turn over to God?

4. "My-oh-my-opia" is another spiritual sight problem that Rhonda describes. She defines it as "worrying and fretting over our future instead of trusting the God who holds it in his hands." What causes "my-oh-my-opia" to affect your spiritual vision?

5. According to the section "Is This Better, or Is This Better," where do we find "corrective lenses" for our spiritual vision problems?

6. Insight gives us the best possible view of God's plan for our lives. What does Rhonda say is the reward when we finally see clearly?

Chapter Eighteen: Mirror, Mirror

1. When Rhonda woke up one morning, she looked in the mirror. In the reflection was an imposter, a woman in Rhonda's jammies who looked disheveled and alien-like stared back at her. Rhonda would prefer to reflect on God and become a reflection of his glory. What does she do on a regular basis to make sure her spiritual life is healthy? How can you apply those principles to your spiritual life?

2. In the section "Reflect on This," Rhonda says, "If I'm walking in the Spirit and living in his love, focusing fully on Christ, then it's a loving spirit of grace and glory that others will see reflecting from my life." What do others see reflecting from your life? Are you happy with that image?

3. Colossians 3 tells us how we have taken off the old self, which Rhonda describes as having "spiritual pillow marks, makeup leftovers, and crazy hair." We are renewed or cleaned up in "knowledge in the image of its Creator." Additionally, Ephesians 4:22–24 says, "You were taught, with regard to your former ways of life, to put off your old self, which is being corrupted by its deceitful desires; to be made new in the attitude of your minds; and to put on the new self, created to be like God in true righteousness and holiness." What is the best way to gain this "knowledge" and "to be made new in the attitude of your minds"?

4. In "It's All about Image" Rhonda quotes 2 Corinthians 3:18 from *The Message*: "And so we are transfigured much like the Messiah, our lives gradually becoming brighter and more beautiful as God enters our lives and we become like him." Which kind of beauty fades with time and which gets "brighter and more beautiful" as we age? How does this concept set you free from our culture's values?

Chapter Nineteen: Wake Up and Smell the Jerky

1. Rhonda has visions of "Java Jerky" being used throughout the country to keep people alert for their jobs, classes, or commute. Being physically alert is a great thing, but spiritual alertness is even better. Why does 1 Peter 5:8 instruct us to be "self-controlled and alert"?

2. In "Stay Perky" Rhonda says we can cast all our cares and anxieties on Jesus, and therefore we are free to do ... what?

3. Near the end of "Stay Perky," Rhonda quotes 1 Thessalonians 5:5–6, 8: "We do not belong to the night or to the darkness. So then, let us not be like others, who are asleep, but let us be alert and self-controlled. ... But since we belong to the day, let us be self-controlled, putting on faith and love as a breastplate, and the hope of salvation

as a helmet." Why do you think this passage and 1 Peter 5:8 pair alertness with self-control? What role does self-control play in learning to love others?

4. What are the things you need to do to "stay alert" in your spiritual life? What is your personal brand of spiritual caffeine?

Chapter Twenty: Clicking for Love in All the Wrong Places

1. Rhonda admits to being a little web-obsessed. It's easy to "get beached" while surfing the net. Rhonda highlights some specific dangers to men and women who are disgruntled with their marriages or singles who have unrealistic love-life fantasies. What are those dangers?

2. The devil is prowling around on the Internet. He is seeking those who are not alert and self-controlled. What are we to do if we are tempted or think evil thoughts while on the Internet (or anywhere else, for that matter)?

3. What are the benefits of the Internet? What are its evils? We can't brand the Internet as "sinful" just because of the obvious ungodly material found on it. We can use it for good, such as sharing the Gospel. If, however, the Internet causes you to sin, you should unplug. What steps have you taken to make sure you and your family are protected from its deceitful lures? Are you aware of the software programs that allow you to check and see where loved ones are "surfing"?

4. Not only is the content on the Internet a potential snare, but the amount of time we spend on the computer can pull us away from the Lord and our families. Rhonda says, "We need to make sure the time we spend (and the *amount* of time we spend) on the computer is God-honoring. Our focus should always be on him." Rhonda knows she's been

spending too much time on the computer when she realizes she hasn't seen her best friends in a long time. What criteria do you have to evaluate if you have a computer addiction? Do you spend time on other things that are dishonoring to God? If so, what can you do to take back control of your time?

Part Five: Surrendering Control in a Control-top World

Chapter Twenty-one: Living a Superwoman Life in an Olive Oyl Body

1. After having five children and living in "Flabsville" ever since, Rhonda has learned where her real strength comes from. Read Isaiah 40:28–31 and Philippians 4:13. In what areas does God offer strength?

2. How do we escape the "wimpy life" and take advantage of God's strength? According to Rhonda, what type of muscles does this require?

3. Ephesians 6:10–17 explains about the armor of God. Against whom or what is our struggle? Will being in good physical shape help us? Which piece of armor do you rely on the most? Which piece do you need to "polish" in order to stand strong against the enemy?

4. By remembering God's past trustworthiness, we can find peace for today's concerns. Get a piece of writing paper and fold it in half. On one side list all the areas in your life that worry you. Now recall the times God has proven himself trustworthy to you—or if you can't think of any, use stories from Scripture that demonstrate his faithfulness. Write those down on the other side of the paper. Compare

the two lists. Is God powerful enough to help you through your current worries? Pray that God will remind you of his strength whenever you encounter trials and temptations.

Chapter Twenty-two: Calendar-itis

1. Losing her appointment calendar helped Rhonda realize she was too dependent on it. "Before we plan our days," she says, "we need to remember that our heavenly Father has plans for us." According to Jeremiah 29:11, what will the Father's plans yield in our lives?

2. In the section "A Calendar with Purpose" Rhonda quotes Rick Warren's *The Purpose Driven® Life*. The book states that if you can't get everything done, you're doing more than God intended for you to do. In order to simplify our lives, what does Mr. Warren suggest we should find out? Do you have a clear-cut spiritual purpose that helps you order your days? Would forming or refining your purpose help you be better focused?

3. Praying and studying the Bible can take up a good chunk of our time. When we're the busiest, we need God the most to help us get everything done with the right attitude. Rhonda notes, "We're better equipped when we've spent time with the Lord in prayer. ... it's essential in those busy times if we want our life to be about the kingdom and not just about the hubbub of a full calendar." What are the most important responsibilities you have right now? Do you sometimes try to accomplish them without prayer? If so, what happens? What are your "kingdom priorities"? Can you accomplish any of those without prayer? Why or why not?

4. The section "Follow the Yellow-Brick Road?" describes a life with no peace, following a road and going "both ways." Rhonda says, "There is, however, great peace in heading down his road of true purpose." Do you know God's true

purpose for your life? Do you need to pull off the road and ponder his plans for you?

Chapter Twenty-three: Drop and Give Him All

1. When Rhonda was at a professional meeting with a book publisher, she glanced down at her nails and noticed she had forgotten to paint one of them. How embarrassing for her to be caught with an unfinished project! While being disciplined at home and work is important, Rhonda says it's more important that we be disciplined in every area of our spiritual lives. Can we be fruitful or successful in our Christian lives if we are undisciplined? According to Romans 7:15–16, which Rhonda quotes in the section "Marching Orders," did the apostle Paul have an easy time acting consistently in spiritual matters?

2. What is in place for us when we "mess up"? Does God ever bully us into obedience when we fail? What does he offer us so that we have the "strength to live the way we were meant to"?

3. There is a great paradox in the Christian life. When we admit our weaknesses is the time when God makes us the strongest. Rhonda quotes Isaiah 40:29 (NKJV) in the section "Strength through Weakness." It says, "He gives power to the weak, and to those who have no might he increases strength." What happens when we admit our weaknesses before our God? If we hold onto pride or a sense of false personal power, what is our fate?

4. What does God require from you, according to Rhonda in the section "For the Purpose of Godliness"? (Hint: Drop and give him ___.) What should be our motivation for becoming spiritually disciplined? How can you tell if you are asking with pure motives?

5. In the section "Pleasing the Commander" Rhonda quotes 2 Timothy 2:4: "No one serving as a soldier gets involved in civilian affairs—he wants to please his commanding officer." What are the competing "civilian affairs" in your life? How can you show God today that you want to please him?

Chapter Twenty-four: More than Meets the Nose

1. Rhonda's not the best cook. One day she was in the kitchen and her friend commented, "Mmm, I love the smell of broccoli cooking." It was a nice compliment, but Rhonda was making pudding, not broccoli. The experience got Rhonda wondering this: If people "sniffed" our spirits, could they tell what we're really made of? If your spiritual life had a fragrance, describe what it would smell like.

2. In the section "Get a Whiff of This" Rhonda says, "As we breathe in the Father and learn to imitate him, we learn really to live a life of love. Learning to imitate him means learning to be surrendered to what he wants for our lives and becoming lovingly obedient to what he wants us to do." What is the key to imitating Christ as outlined in 2 John 1:5?

3. In the section "Walking in Love" Rhonda says, "I want my life to be a fragrant offering as I learn to obediently walk in his commands." Through obedience, we learn to walk in love. In which areas of your life do you need to become more obedient? If you surrender those areas to God, how will that make you a more loving person?

4. This chapter ends with 2 John 1:3–7 from *The Message*. Verse 5 says, "But permit me a reminder, friends, and this is not a new commandment but simply a repetition of our original and basic charter: that we love each other." Everyone needs reminders to love. Do you attend Bible studies? Do you have a prayer/accountability partner?

What are some steps you can take to ensure that you are obediently pursuing love?

Chapter Twenty-five: Cut and Dry

1. Whenever Rhonda needs a haircut, she goes to an expert. She has tried to cut her own bangs with disastrous results. She notes a similarity between submitting to a hairstylist and submitting to God. She says, "Doesn't it make more sense to leave the life-controlling to the expert? You know, the one who designed life in the first place?" When Rhonda takes control of her life, what does she say happens every time? When you are not allowing God to lead you, what are the results?

2. In the section "The 'Shear' Facts" Rhonda says, "We please God and show our love for him by surrendering to the scissors, so to speak, in complete obedience. She then quotes John 14:15. According to this verse, how can we show God that we love him?

3. The passages John 15:10–11 and John 14:21 reveal the results of an obedient life. Read the verses and make a list of the positive results of following God's commands.

   Are you lacking joy in your life? What steps can you take so that you feel "more at home" and joyful in God's presence?

4. "Father controls best" is a phrase Rhonda uses in this chapter. To our "cultured" ears, this may sound un-American or anti-woman. Which mores of our society do you think would go against the "Father controls best" philosophy? What areas of your thinking do you need to adjust in order to be fully obedient to a "controlling" God?

Part Six: Maid to Order

Chapter Twenty-six: I'm a Little Teapot

1. Rhonda reminds us through the childhood song "I'm a Little Teapot" that God crafted and shaped us to be exactly who we are. She says, "[God] didn't get to the finished project and say, 'Oh, no! I was trying for a teapot on this one.'" What happens if we allow ourselves to be discontent with how God made us? According to Rhonda, what happens when "the teapot surrenders to the purpose its designer had in mind?"

2. Rhonda quotes Ephesians 4:1–3 from *The Message*. In that passage, the apostle Paul wrote that we should be "pouring ourselves out for each other in acts of love." Further in the verse, he describes two of those love acts. What are they?

3. In the section "Spilling Out Love" Rhonda notes when we are serving others, we are accomplishing something else as well. What is it? (Hint: See Ephesians 6:7.)

4. Loving service requires humility. Rhonda says, "It's pride that causes us to look at someone else's gifts and abilities and think that we should be called to serve in the same way. First Corinthians 12:4 says that 'There are different kinds of gifts, but the same Spirit.'" Which gifts God has given you? Are you content with those gifts? As you mature, what do you envision God doing with your gifts and your life?

5. Rhonda suggests we pray like this: "Lord, fill us up with you—then tip us over and pour us out! Use us to serve in every big way and every small way that will bring glory and honor to you." How will that prayer help you to discover or solidify your purpose in Christ?

Chapter Twenty-seven: Choose This Day

1. The whole theme of this chapter is choice. Rhonda gets to choose her face cream. She can choose for whom to vote. She also gets to choose whether or not she will serve God. "The choice is ours," she says. "Let's not blow it. ... Joshua 24:15 says: 'But if serving the LORD seems undesirable to you, then choose for yourselves this day whom you will serve.'" If you are not serving God, who are you really serving? What are those things, people, or idols you may be tempted to serve instead of God? Has there been a time in your life when you chose to serve yourself instead of God? What were the results?

2. The section "Choosy Christians Choose Service" tells a little about Joshua and the people of Israel. Rhonda says, "The people [the Israelites] were free to choose, but 'not deciding' was not an option. To choose any way other than God's way was to choose self." Is it the same for us today? Why or why not?

3. How can you make a clear choice to serve God today? What action can you take that shows you and your household serve the Lord?

4. According to Deuteronomy 10:12–13, what does God expect from you?

Chapter Twenty-eight: Tweeze the Day

1. In this chapter Rhonda laments she does so much upper-lip tweezing all the blood runs out of her arms. She has to tweeze every day to make sure a moustache doesn't grow under her nose. Making the most out of life requires the same diligence. What does Rhonda say is one of the secrets to making the most out of life?

2. In the section "Know When to Make a Pit Stop" Rhonda says, "Our bodies require rest, and we can serve him better when we give our bodies what they need. As a matter of fact, we can even serve him in our resting." To what extent is this statement true? How do we balance rest with pursuing God with zeal and passion?

3. Rhonda discusses that staying excited in the Lord can help us make the most of every opportunity. Ephesians 5:15–16 (MSG) says, "Watch your step. Use your head. Make the most of every chance you get." What are some practical ways to do this? Do you know people who make the most of every opportunity? What do you think is their secret?

4. This chapter ends with Galatians 6:7–10 (MSG). Verse 10 says, "Right now, therefore, every time we get the chance, let us work for the benefit of all, starting with the people closest to us in the community of faith." What are you doing to serve your church today? If you don't have a specific assignment or task at your church, what are some helpful things you can start doing to "work for the benefit of all"?

Chapter Twenty-nine: Runners in the Stockings of Life

1. You can bank on this: As soon as you think you're dressed and ready to go out the door, you hit a snag—in your only good pair of pantyhose. "Our spiritual lives can hit the same kind of snags," Rhonda says. "We have so much we'd like to accomplish for the Lord. We see things moving along at a good clip in our service for Christ when, RIP!— a major runner-like interruption." What are some of the snags or interruptions you've encountered in your spiritual life? How did they impact your service to Christ?

2. When—not if—those trials come, what does 1 Peter 4:19 as quoted in the section "The Tough Keep Running" tell us to do? Do you agree with this kind of outlook? Why or why not?

3. Does God notice when we keep on serving despite rotten circumstances? Of course! Can you think of individuals who are an example of this "runner-like" service? Do you aspire to persevere like them? Why or why not?

4. Rhonda notes, "Not only does the Lord notice our perseverance when difficulties come along, but on top of it all, he even uses those very difficulties to build more perseverance and maturity." Explain the testing/maturity formula as outlined in James 1:2–4.

5. According to the section "Joy in the Snags" what reward awaits those who arrive at spiritual maturity?

Chapter Thirty: Taking the Plunge

1. The Bible tells us to "plunge in" to service. The illustration Rhonda uses for this chapter is wading through a disgusting toilet overflow pool to stop the filth from spreading. Do you hesitate to serve if the task seems too difficult or unpleasant? Why do people admire Christians who serve "in the trenches"?

2. "Whatever our situation," Rhonda says, "one thing is clear: We're supposed to be serving. ... Not one of us is left out of the charge. Each one has received a gift. Each one needs to be using that gift in service for Christ." List things you've done for the Lord that you enjoyed doing. What do you think one or more of your spiritual gifts are?

3. According to 1 Timothy 4:14–16, what is the result of service to the Lord? Can you see that principle at work in your life? In the lives of others?

4. Rhonda calls God the "heavenly Head Hunter." What does she recommend for those who are searching for a ministry? What are your plans for beginning or continuing in a ministry?

Part Seven: Grace To Go

Chapter Thirty-one: True Grit

1. The theme of this chapter is the value of salt. Rhonda is in the habit of asking these questions related to being "the salt of the earth." What are your personal answers to the following:

* Am I spicing up life for those around me?
* Am I having a purifying effect on the people I meet?
* Am I encouraging others to thirst for Jesus?
* Am I allowing God to use me to preserve life, or am I ignoring the spiritual death in those I encounter every day?
* Am I allowing the Lord to use my saltiness to show off his good works and bring glory to him, or am I just empty grit?

2. Three body fluids are key examples in understanding the role of salt in our spiritual lives. The first mentioned is tears. What do you treasure enough to cry about? What can your tears show God? How does God view tears?

3. The second example is sweat, the result of work. What does 1 Corinthians 15:58 say about work and labor in the Christian life?

4. The last example is blood. People are called to bleed—the ultimate sacrifice. Are you willing to sacrifice yourself if it means your heavenly Father will be glorified? Can you abandon all, knowing you belong to the Lord?

Chapter Thirty-two: Shoe—mania

1. The theme of this chapter is shoes, feet, and where they should be headed. God's Word says in Isaiah, "How beautiful on the mountains are the feet of those who bring good news" (52:7). Do you agree with Rhonda that "Sharing the Good News is more satisfying than a bargain pair of shoes"? Why or why not?

2. Sharing the Good News is foundational for completing our "spiritual look." Are you leaving out the "sharing Christ" part of your spiritual life? If so, what does Rhonda say you're missing as a result?

3. Have you ever asked yourself what kind of shoe you might be? Look at the section "Foot-notes." Do any of the shoe types listed "fit" your evangelism style? Which pair of shoes would you like to become a perfect fit?

4. Read Ephesians 6:13–17, paying particular attention to verse 15, which says, "And with your feet fitted with the readiness that comes from the gospel of peace." Can you put this verse into your own words? Are your feet "fitted with the readiness"? Can you be a completely armored Christian without this element? Why or why not?

Chapter Thirty-three: The Perfect Gift

1. Rhonda's a ripper. She loves gifts and tears the wrapping paper right off, and she says that her spiritual gift is "receiving." Being a connoisseur of fine gifts, she thinks it's unimaginable that some people don't receive the gift of salvation through Jesus Christ. In the section "The Most Expensive Gift Ever" Rhonda cites two reasons for people refusing the gift of Life. What are they? Can you think of any other reasons people might refuse God's gift?

2. What does Rhonda want us to remember, even more than the date of her birthday (which is, by the way, March 20!)? What are the two ways we can help people understand the Gospel? Is sharing the Gospel enough? Why or why not? Is living the gospel enough? Why or why not?

3. Rhonda quotes James 1:17: "Every good and perfect gift is from above, coming down from the Father of the heavenly lights." She says, "[God] fills our lives with meaning, grants us undeserved grace and love, infuses us with joy, and then gives us a charge. For us gals, it's sort of like the ultimate 'You go, girl.'"

   What other gifts has the Father given to you? Is there any good thing in this world that did not come from God?

4. At the end of this chapter, Matthew 28:19–20 from *The Message* is quoted. Our charge from Jesus is "Go out and train everyone you meet, far and near, in this way of life, marking them by baptism in the threefold name: Father, Son, and Holy Spirit. Then instruct them in the practice of all I have commanded you. I'll be with you as you do this, day after day after day, right up to the end of the age." With this charge, Jesus gives us a promise. What is it? Do you really trust Jesus to be with you as you serve him? How does this promise empower you to follow the charge?

Chapter Thirty-four: To-Go Order

1. If you drive through a take-out window, of course your food order is "to-go"—Rhonda discovered this fact one day after placing an order at a fast-food restaurant. It's a given. In the same way, Jesus' order for us "to go" into the world Matthew 28:19–20 is as obvious. At the end of the section "Make That to Go" Rhonda describes two types of "to-go" orders. What are they?

2. Abraham was commanded to do a "movement" to-go. What was his response that led to his being mentioned in the Hebrews hall of fame? Have you ever had a to-go order from God? What was your response?

3. In the section "Blessing in Going" Rhonda says, "It's good to remember that when we're immediately obedient, there is blessing" and "Radical obedience equals radical blessing." Have you seen this principle at work in your life? What about in the lives of others? Do you think she's exaggerating the importance of obedience, or is this an accurate portrayal of the Christian life?

4. Are you a good candidate for a "to-go" order from God? Why or why not? Are there distractions in your life that keep you from obeying? If so, what are they? What would it take for you to boldly go wherever God asked you?

5. In Luke 10:2 Jesus said, "The harvest is plentiful, but the workers are few. Ask the Lord of the harvest, therefore, to send out workers into his harvest field." Are you committed to pray for "to-go" orders and be a worker for God? Do you pray regularly for Christians to go and preach to all nations? What else can you do to help with the harvest?

Chapter Thirty-five: For the Love of Chocolate

1. Rhonda opens this chapter with a tribute to chocolate—the waxy kind. She says, "There's hardly anything better than a good friend and some semi-good chocolate. It's some of life's sweetest sharing." The ultimate sharing, however, is sharing the good news of our salvation. Do you agree that sharing the Good News is the ultimate in good? Why or why not?

2. What must we first understand to ensure we have "the best way to share the message of salvation"? Why is this concept so important and so freeing?

3. In the section "Go Prayed Up" Rhonda encourages us to wrap our witnessing in prayer. She quotes 1 Timothy 2:4–8 (MSG). According to this passage what is "at the bottom" of sharing the Gospel?

4. The apostle Paul asked for prayer that the Lord would bring opportunities for him to share Jesus in prison (Col. 4:3). What unlikely place might God want you to share? Do you have a unique opportunity to share the Gospel message that other Christians don't have? Are you committed to praying for evangelism opportunities to come your way?

5. Rhonda suggests asking unbelievers questions about their faith as a good conversation starter. What are some of the "good" questions she recommends? How do you know when to back off so you're not viewed as pushy? If you're sharing with someone who's not willing to listen, what should you do?

6. Name the three verses found in the section "Share Simply" that are good for introducing the Gospel to newcomers. Are you willing to practice paraphrasing those verses so that they sound simple and honest, not like a prepared speech?

7. What should you do if someone you talk with makes a decision to become a Christian? (Besides jumping up and down and celebrating by eating twenty Ding Dongs!)

Part Nine: The Rest of the Story

Chapter Thirty-six: Flap-happy

1. The theme of this chapter is wind and what happens when it comes into our lives. How does Rhonda describe the relationship between the wind and a soaring eagle? What keeps the eagle in flight? How is that analogous to our lives when we rest in Christ?

2. Rhonda quotes Exodus 19:3–4 in the section "When Soaring Gets Tough." Read this passage and answer: How does God describe how he helped the Israelites out of Egypt? When the ride gets rough in our spiritual lives, how does God help us? Describe a time in your life when the Lord "carried you on eagles' wings" and gave you rest during turbulent times.

3. Rhonda says, "There's no safer place to be than resting in our faithful Father." She quotes Matthew 11:28–29 (HSCB), "Come to Me, all you who are weary and burdened, and I will give you rest. Take My yoke upon you and learn from Me, because I am gentle and humble in heart, and you will find rest for your souls." What can we do when we're feeling spiritually wimpy? Is your concept of the Father one of gentleness? Why or why not? How does this verse encourage you to trust Jesus without fear?

4. In *The Message* Matthew 11:30 reads, "Keep company with me and you'll learn to live freely and lightly." What are some ways we can "keep company" with Jesus? Describe how you would like to "live freely and lightly."

Chapter Thirty-seven: I'll Fly Away

1. The theme of this chapter is fear. We don't have anything to fear when we're with Jesus—even a "purgatory-type" airplane flight. In the section "Truly Secure Flight,"

Rhonda quotes John 10:27–29. Read this passage and explain why it offers comfort to you.

2. We need to have our hearts firmly planted in the love of Christ according to Ephesians 3:18. Doing this will enable us to "take in with all Christians the extravagant dimensions of Christ's love." Describe an instance in your life when you felt the "extravagant" love of Christ. If you can't recall a special moment, what do you imagine it would feel like?

3. What are your personal fears? How can the love of Christ comfort you today? What are your goals for allowing Jesus to lift you beyond those fears? List two Bible verses you can meditate on to help you toward this goal. How can you help or encourage someone else who is bound by fear?

Chapter Thirty-eight: Not by Sight

1. We live by faith, not by sight—so the sight of Rhonda in ill-fitting jeans doesn't really matter when eternity is foremost in our minds. What does matter is faith. Is it possible to please God without faith according to Hebrews 11: 6? Why or why not?

2. Hebrews 11:1 says, "Now faith is being sure of what we hope for and certain of what we do not see." Describe your faith—what do you believe about God that you can't touch, taste, hear, or smell?

3. Where does faith come from, according to Hebrews 12:2? What temporary obstacles prevent you from fixing your eyes on Jesus? Whose job is it to take our obedience (the "fixing" part) and perfect our faith?

4. How often do we need to be renewed in our faith? What does the Lord do for us when we remain faithful? According

to Rhonda, are we to worry about our outward self? Why is the inner self so much more important to God?

Chapter Thirty-nine: Christian Soup for the Chicken Soul

1. Rhonda thinks that shows like *Fear Factor* should include some truly scary stunts for moms, such as a husband inviting spur-of-the-moment guests over after church on Sunday. Actually, we don't have to be fearful at all. Being a believer gives us the ability to "trade fear for peace when we trade fret and worry for prayer." Are there fears in your life that you need to trade in for peace? Tell about a time when you were fearful and God offered protection through prayer.

2. Describe how being "prayer-shaped" can change your perspective on momentary fears. How does this allow God to "settle us down," according to Philippians 4:7 (MSG)?

3. In the section "The Real Courage Factor" Rhonda reminds us about the great apostle Peter who was afraid to stand up for Jesus. After he received the Holy Spirit, however, Peter became a bold preacher. Rhonda says he went "from wimpy zero to fearless hero." Have you ever been afraid to stand up for Jesus? What do you need in order to combat fear?

4. What is the good kind of fear, according to Proverbs 19:23? Describe what the fear of God is in your own words. What is the difference between good fear and bad fear?

5. Psalm 112:6–8 tells us we don't even have to be nervous. What other privileges mentioned in this verse are available for the righteous woman?

Chapter Forty: Nine Lives

1. Rhonda's cat is undeserving of love. It makes a mess, coughs up hairballs, and worse, has a bad attitude. But undeserving as it is, her children love the cat. It's the same way with God and us. Rhonda says, "[God] loves and wants you so much that even though you were separated from him by sin, he made a plan to win you back." What was the plan to win us back according to Romans 5:8 and 3:23–25?

2. Romans 10:13 promises, "Everyone who calls on the name of the Lord will be saved." Rhonda says, "His unconditional, selfless, sacrificing, extravagant love has made new life possible for all who will receive him—eternal life." Is this easy to believe? Why or why not? Rhonda also says, "God loves us without strings." Do you see any strings attached to God's promise of eternal life? If so, what are those strings tied to? What can you do to loosen those strings so you can freely believe?

3. If you haven't already, would you like to get in on the "forever life"? If so, let Jesus know about it by praying. Rhonda offers a sample prayer in the last section of this chapter.

4. The last verse quoted in this book is Ephesians 1:11 from *The Message:* "It's in Christ that we find out who we are and what we are living for." In light of this verse, who are you? What are you living for today? What tools has this book given you so that your life can be filled more and more with Jesus?

*It's in Christ that we find out
who we are and what we are living for.*

Ephesians 1:11, THE MESSAGE

The Word at Work . . .

What would you do if you wanted to share God's love with children on the streets of your city? That's the dilemma David C. Cook faced in 1870s Chicago. His answer was to create literature that would capture children's hearts.

Out of those humble beginnings grew a worldwide ministry that has used literature to proclaim God's love and disciple generation after generation. Cook Communications Ministries is committed to personal discipleship—to helping people of all ages learn God's Word, embrace his salvation, walk in his ways, and minister in his name.

Opportunities—and Crisis

We live in a land of plenty—including plenty of Christian literature! But what about the rest of the world? Jesus commanded, "Go and make disciples of all nations" (Matt. 28:19) and we want to obey this commandment. But how does a publishing organization "go" into all the world?

There are five times as many Christians around the world as there are in North America. Christian workers in many of these countries have no more than a New Testament, or perhaps a single shared copy of the Bible, from which to learn and teach.

We are committed to sharing what God has given us with such Christians.

A vital part of Cook Communications Ministries is our international outreach, Cook Communications Ministries International (CCMI). Your purchase of this book, and of other books and Christian-growth products from Cook, enables CCMI to provide Bibles and Christian literature to people in more than 150 languages in 65 countries.

Cook Communications Ministries is a not-for-profit, self-supporting organization. Revenues from sales of our books, Bible curricula, and other church and home products not only fund our U.S. ministry, but also fund our CCMI ministry around the world. One hundred percent of donations to CCMI go to our international literature programs.

. . . Around the World

CCMI reaches out internationally in three ways:

· Our premier International Christian Publishing Institute (ICPI) trains leaders from nationally led publishing houses around the world to develop evangelism and discipleship materials to transform lives in their countries.

· We provide literature for pastors, evangelists, and Christian workers in their national language. We provide study helps for pastors and lay leaders in many parts of the world, such as China, India, Cuba, Iran, and Vietnam.

· We reach people at risk—refugees, AIDS victims, street children, and famine victims—with God's Word. CCMI puts literature that shares the Good News into the hands of people at spiritual risk—people who might die before they hear the name of Jesus and are transformed by his love.

Word Power, God's Power

Faith Kidz, RiverOak, Honor, Life Journey, Victor, NexGen — every time you purchase a book produced by Cook Communications Ministries, you not only meet a vital personal need in your life or in the life of someone you love, but you're also a part of ministering to José in Colombia, Humberto in Chile, Gousa in India, or Lidiane in Brazil. You help make it possible for a pastor in China, a child in Peru, or a mother in West Africa to enjoy a life-changing book. And because you helped, children and adults around the world are learning God's Word and walking in his ways.

Thank you for your partnership in helping to disciple the world. May God bless you with the power of his Word in your life.

For more information about our
international ministries, visit www.ccmi.org.

Additional copies of *TURKEY SOUP FOR THE SOUL*
are available from your local bookseller.

• • • • •

If you have enjoyed this book,
or if it has had an impact on your life,
we would like to hear from you.

Please contact us at:

LIFE JOURNEY
Cook Communications Ministries, Dept. 201
4050 Lee Vance View
Colorado Springs, CO 80918
Or at our Web site: www.cookministries.com

LIFE JOURNEY®
Bringing Home the Message for Life